Nancy Bacevich

ANDREW J. BACEVICH, a professor of history and international relations at Boston University, served for
twenty-three years as an officer in the U.S. Army. He is
the author of *Washington Rules*, *The Limits of Power*,
and *The New American Militarism*, among other books.
His writing has appeared in *Foreign Affairs*, *The Atlantic*, *Harper's*, *The Nation*, and *The New York Times*.

ALSO BY ANDREW J. BACEVICH

The Short American Century:
A Postmortem (editor)

Washington Rules:
America's Path to Permanent War

The Limits of Power:
The End of American Exceptionalism

The Long War: A New History of
U.S. National Security Policy Since World War II (editor)

The New American Militarism:
How Americans Are Seduced by War

American Empire:
The Realities and Consequences of U.S. Diplomacy

The Imperial Tense:
Prospects and Problems of American Empire (editor)

Additional Praise for *Breach of Trust*

"Bacevich offers a brilliant critique of an American military system sharply at variance with our democratic republican ideals. Most disturbing is his compelling argument that the fault lies with We the People. A thought-provoking ride." —Karl W. Eikenberry, Lieutenant General, U.S. Army (Retired) and former U.S. Ambassador to Afghanistan

"*Breach of Trust* addresses a fundamental numbness pervading the country. . . . This scathing critique of America's state of permanent war is not to be missed by anyone who understands—or suspects that there's something going terribly wrong here." —*Los Angeles Review of Books*

"Gripping, appropriately lacerating . . . perhaps [his] angriest book." —*Bookforum*

"Bacevich makes a powerful and deeply necessary case for a fundamental shift in the way that we fight our wars." —*The Daily Beast*

"With American warmongers and militarists demanding the bombing of North Korea and intervention in the Syrian civil war, Andrew Bacevich's powerfully written *Breach of Trust* comes at a critical time. For Bacevich, the problem is perpetual war, a condition fostered by our citizens' detachment from the conflicts America fights. President Obama, Congress, and the Joint Chiefs of Staff should read this book, but the American people *must* read it because they, to Bacevich, represent the solution." —Colonel Gian P. Gentile, associate professor of history, West Point

"A mixture of passion, dismay, and cynicism, with streaks of perhaps hopeless hope." —*Kirkus Reviews*

"In this provocative book, Bacevich traces a dangerous shift in the relationship between the military and the American people.... A sweeping condemnation of the sins that have been wrought because of the American people's willingness to wash their hands of the costs of war."   —*The Christian Century*

"A powerful critique of U.S. foreign policy."   —*Reason*

"Like the soldier that he was, Andrew Bacevich is courageous. As the scholar that he is, he is learned. As a citizen, he is impassioned. All this has combined to produce a unique voice of great value in American political life. In *Breach of Trust,* he anatomizes what he knows best, the acute danger our current military institutions and policies pose to American democracy. Anyone who cherishes that democracy should read and heed this book."

—Jonathan Schell, author of
The Unconquerable World and *The Real War*

"*Breach of Trust* is grimly eloquent, with prose as effortless as its truths are hard. In this superb history, Andrew Bacevich reveals the civil-military dysfunction that made this a nation of endless conflicts, waged by a professional warrior class, for a public that has traded civic virtue for mindless flag-waving. This is an original, provocative, and invaluable book for anyone who hasn't given up on America."   —Nick Turse, author of *Kill Anything That Moves: The Real American War in Vietnam*

"An impassioned and painfully convincing polemic ... Bacevich asserts bluntly that a disengaged and compliant citizenry has reduced military service from a universal duty to a matter of individual choice, allowing our leaders to wage war whenever (and for however long) they choose."   —*Publishers Weekly* (starred review)

BREACH

OF

TRUST

HOW AMERICANS FAILED THEIR
SOLDIERS AND THEIR COUNTRY

ANDREW J. BACEVICH

PICADOR   A METROPOLITAN BOOK   HENRY HOLT AND COMPANY   NEW YORK

www.picadorusa.com
www.twitter.com/picadorusa • www.facebook.com/picadorusa
picadorbookroom.tumblr.com

Picador® is a U.S. registered trademark and is used by Metropolitan Books
under license from Pan Books Limited.

For book club information, please visit www.facebook.com/picadorbookclub
or e-mail marketing@picadorusa.com.

Designed by Kelly Too

The Library of Congress has cataloged the Henry Holt edition as follows:

Bacevich, Andrew J.
    Breach of trust : how Americans failed their soldiers and their country /
Andrew J. Bacevich.—1st ed.
        p. cm.
Includes bibliographical references and index.
ISBN 978-0-8050-8296-8 (hardcover)
ISBN 978-0-8050-9603-3 (e-book)
    1. War and society—United States.   2. National security—Social aspects—United
States.   3. Military Service, Voluntary—United States.   4. Sacrifice—Social aspects—
United States.   5. Citizenship—Social—United States.   6. United States—History,
Military—20th century.   7. United States—History, Military—21st century.   I. Title.
E181.B15 2013
355.00973—dc23   2013004885

Picador ISBN 978-1-250-05538-5

Picador books may be purchased for educational, business, or promotional use.
For information on bulk purchases, please contact Macmillan Corporate
and Premium Sales Department at 1-800-221-7945, extension 5442,
or write specialmarkets@macmillan.com.

First published in the United States by Metropolitan Books,
an imprint of Henry Holt and Company

First Picador Edition: September 2014

10 9 8 7 6 5 4 3 2 1

To my sisters and my brothers
with love and gratitude

and

To the memory of
Captain William F. Reichert
and
Colonel Theodore S. Westhusing

In the purer ages of the commonwealth, the use of arms was reserved for . . . citizens who had a country to love, a property to defend, and some share in enacting those laws which it was in their interest, as well as duty, to maintain. But as the public freedom was lost in extent of conquest, war was gradually improved into an art, and degraded into a trade . . . That public virtue which among the ancients was denominated patriotism derived from a strong sense of interest in the preservation of free government . . . Such a sentiment . . . could make but a very feeble impression on the mercenary servants of a despotic prince.

Edward Gibbon,
The Decline and Fall of the Roman Empire

CONTENTS

BREACH OF TRUST

PROLOGUE

Fenway Park, Boston, July 4, 2011. On this warm, summer day the Red Sox will play the Toronto Blue Jays. First, however, come pre-game festivities especially tailored for the occasion. The ensuing spectacle—a carefully scripted encounter between the armed forces and society—expresses the distilled essence of present-day American patriotism. A masterpiece of contrived spontaneity, the event leaves spectators feeling good about their baseball team, about their military, and not least of all about themselves—precisely as it was meant to do.

In this theatrical production, the Red Sox provide the stage, and the Pentagon the props. In military parlance, it is a joint operation. In front of a gigantic American flag draped over the left-field wall, an air force contingent, clad in blue, stands at attention. To carry a smaller version of the Stars and Stripes onto the playing field, the navy provides a color guard in crisp summer whites. The U.S. Marine Corps kicks in with a choral ensemble that leads the singing of the national anthem. As its final notes sound, four U.S. Air Force F-15C Eagles scream overhead. The sellout crowd roars its approval.

But there is more to come. "On this Independence Day," the voice of the Red Sox booms over the public address system, "we pay a debt of gratitude to the families whose sons and daughters are serving our country." On this occasion, the designated recipients of that gratitude are members of the Lydon family, hailing from Squantum, Massachusetts. Young Bridget Lydon is a sailor—Aviation Ordnanceman Airman is her official title—serving aboard the carrier USS *Ronald Reagan*, currently deployed in support of the Afghanistan War.

The Lydons are Every Family, decked out for the Fourth. Garbed in random bits of Red Sox paraphernalia and Mardi Gras necklaces, they wear their shirts untucked and ball caps backward. Neither sleek nor fancy, they are without pretension. Yet they exude good cheer. As they are ushered onto the field, their eagerness is palpable. Like TV game show contestants, they know that their lucky day has finally arrived, and they are keen to make the most of it.

As the Lydons gather near the pitcher's mound, the voice directs their attention to the 38-by-100-foot Jumbotron mounted above the center-field bleachers. On the screen, Bridget appears. She is aboard ship, in duty uniform, posed belowdecks in front of an F/A-18 fighter jet. Waiflike, but pert and confident, she looks directly into the camera, sending a "shout-out" to family and friends. She wishes she could join them at Fenway.

As if by magic, wish becomes fulfillment. While the video clip is still running, Bridget herself, now in dress whites, emerges from behind the flag covering the left-field wall. On the Jumbotron, in place of Bridget belowdecks, an image of Bridget marching smartly toward the infield appears. In the stands pandemonium erupts. After a moment of confusion, members of her family—surrounded by camera crews—rush to embrace their sailor, a reunion shared vicariously by the thirty-eight thousand fans in attendance along with many thousands more watching on the Red Sox television network.

Once the Lydons finish with hugs and kisses and the crowd settles down, navy veteran Bridget (annual salary approximately $22,000) throws the ceremonial first pitch to aging Red Sox veteran Tim Wakefield (annual salary—modest for a big leaguer—$2 million). More cheers. As a souvenir, Wakefield gives her the baseball along with a hug of his own. All smiles, Bridget and her family shout "Play Ball!" into a microphone. As they are escorted off the field and out of sight, the game begins.

What does this event signify?

For the Lydons, the day will no doubt long remain a happy memory. If they were to some degree manipulated—their utter and genuine astonishment at Bridget's seemingly miraculous appearance lending the occasion its emotional punch—they played their allotted roles without complaint and with considerable élan. However briefly, they stood in the spotlight, quasi celebrities, the center of attention. Here was a twenty-first-century version of the American dream fulfilled. And if offstage puppet masters used Bridget herself, at least she got a visit home and a few days off—no doubt a welcome break.

Yet this feel-good story had a political as well as a personal dimension. As a collaboration between two well-heeled but image-conscious institutions, the Lydon reunion represented a small but not inconsequential public relations triumph. The Red Sox and the Pentagon had collaborated to perform an act of kindness for a sailor and her loved ones. Both organizations came away looking good—not only because the event itself was so deftly executed, but because it showed that a large for-profit professional sports team and an even larger military bureaucracy both care about ordinary people. The message conveyed to fans/taxpayers could not be clearer: the corporate executives who run the Red Sox have a heart. So, too, do the admirals who run the navy.

Better still, these benefits accrued at essentially no cost to the sponsors. The military personnel arrayed around Fenway showed up because they were told to do so. They are already "paid for," as are the F-15s, the pilots who fly them, and the ground crews that service them. As for whatever outlays the Red Sox may have made, they were trivial and easily absorbed. For the 2011 season, the average price of a ticket at Fenway Park had climbed to fifty-two dollars. A soft drink in a commemorative plastic cup ran you five and a half bucks and a beer eight dollars. Then there was the television ad revenue, all contributing the previous year to corporate profits exceeding $58 million. A decade of war culminating in the worst economic crisis since the Great Depression hadn't done much good for the country, but it had been strangely good for the Red Sox—and an equally well-funded Pentagon. Any money expended in bringing Bridget to Fenway and entertaining the Lydons amounted to the baseball/military equivalent of pocket change.

The holiday festivities at Fenway had a further significance, one that extended beyond burnishing institutional reputations and boosting bottom lines. Here was America's civic religion made manifest. In recent decades, an injunction to "support the troops" has emerged as its central tenet. Since 9/11 this imperative has become, if anything, even more binding. Indeed, as citizens, Americans today acknowledge no higher obligation.

Fulfilling that obligation has posed a challenge, however. Rather than doing so concretely, Americans—with a few honorable exceptions—have settled for symbolism. With a pronounced aversion to collective service and sacrifice (an inclination indulged by leaders of both political parties), Americans resist any definition of civic duty that threatens to crimp lifestyles.

To stand in symbolic solidarity at a ballpark with those on whom the burden of service and sacrifice falls is about as far as they will go—just far enough, that is, to affirm that the existing relationship between the military and society, along with the distribution of privileges and responsibilities that the relationship entails, is congruent with democratic practice. The message that citizens wish to convey to their soldiers is this: although choosing not to be *with* you, we are still *for* you (so long as being for you entails nothing on our part). Cheering for the troops, in effect, provides a convenient mechanism for voiding obligation and perhaps easing guilty consciences.

In ways far more satisfying than displaying banners or bumper stickers, the Fenway Park Independence Day event provided a made-to-order opportunity for conscience easing. It did so in three ways. First, it brought members of Red Sox Nation into close proximity, even if not direct contact, with living, breathing members of the armed forces, figuratively closing any gap between the two. (In New England, where few active duty military installations remain, such encounters are increasingly infrequent.) Second, it manufactured one excuse after another to whistle and shout, whoop and holler, thereby allowing the assembled multitudes to express—and to be seen expressing—their affection and respect for the troops. Finally, it rewarded participants and witnesses alike with a sense of validation, the reunion of Bridget and her family, even if temporary, serving as a proxy for a much larger, if imaginary, reconciliation of the American military and the American people. That debt? Mark it paid in full.

INTRODUCTION

When war claims a soldier's life, what does that death signify? Almost reflexively, Americans want to believe that those making the supreme sacrifice thereby advance the cause of freedom. Since freedom by common consent qualifies as the ultimate American value, death ennobles the fallen soldier.

Yet sometimes nobility is difficult to discern and the significance of a particular death proves elusive. Consider the case of Captain William F. Reichert, shot and killed on January 27, 1971, at An Khe in the Republic of Vietnam. Captain Reichert did not fall in battle. He was assassinated. His assassin was an American soldier.

Age twenty-three, unmarried, and a graduate of West Point's Class of 1968, Reichert was at the time commanding Troop C, First Squadron, Tenth Cavalry. As it happened, I was also stationed at An Khe then, serving as a platoon leader in Troop D.

Despite an impressive lineage, by the time I arrived, the First Squadron, Tenth Cavalry ("Buffalo Soldiers") rated as something other than a "crack" outfit. By the winter of 1970–71, the dwindling

American order of battle in Vietnam boasted few crack outfits. The U.S. Army was heading toward the exits, and those units that remained made for a motley collection.

Higher headquarters had assigned One-Ten Cav the mission of securing a long stretch of highway running west from the coastal city of Qui Nhon through the Central Highlands and on to Pleiku. The squadron's area of operations included the Mang Yang Pass, where in 1954 the Vietminh had obliterated the French army's Groupement Mobile 100, thereby ringing down the curtain on the First Indochina War.[1]

No such replay of the Little Bighorn punctuated my own tour of duty. Indeed, the operative idea—widely understood even if unwritten—was to avoid apocalyptic encounters so that the ongoing drawdown could continue. As long as the withdrawal of U.S. forces proceeded on schedule, authorities in Washington could sustain the pretense that the Second Indochina War was ending in something other than failure.

One-Ten Cav had been allotted little more than a bit part in this elaborate production. Keeping that highway open allowed daily supply convoys to move food, fuel, ammunition, and other essentials to Pleiku and points beyond. To accomplish this mundane task, Buffalo Soldiers in armored vehicles guarded bridges or reacted to enemy ambushes. Others, in helicopters or on foot, conducted reconnaissance patrols, flying above or trudging through the jungle. The assignment offered little by way of glory or grandeur, both of which were then, in any case, in short supply throughout South Vietnam. That late in the war, navigating between honor and dishonor, foolhardy courage and craven cowardice, necessary subordination and mindless obedience posed challenges. It was not a happy time or place to be an American soldier.

Yet if the squadron did not literally share G. M. 100's fate, it was succumbing incrementally to a defeat that was hardly less decisive. As any home owner will tell you, a leaky roof, if left unattended, can pose as much danger as a category five hurricane. Collapse is just a longer time coming. In the backwater that was An Khe, the roof was leaking like a sieve.

No one was likely to mistake the United States in 1971 for a land of concord and contentment. During the interval between the assassination of John F. Kennedy and the election of Richard M. Nixon, cleavages dividing left and right, black and white, flag burners and flag wavers, college kids and working stiffs had become particularly acute. Looming in the background was an even more fundamental cleavage between state and country. Depending on which camp you occupied, the government appeared either clueless or gutless. In any case, those exercising political authority no longer commanded the respect or deference they had enjoyed during the 1940s and 1950s. Sullen citizens eyed their government with cynicism and mistrust.

Comparable division and discord pervaded the ranks of those sent to serve in Vietnam. In the war zone, the animosity between the governing and the governed at home found its parallel in the relationship between leaders and led. In Vietnam, sullen enlisted soldiers—predominantly draftees—eyed their officers with cynicism and mistrust.

To vent their anger at policies not to their liking, outraged citizens engaged in acts of protest. To express their animus toward leaders not to their liking, alienated soldiers did likewise, their acts of protest ranging from disrespect to shirking to out-and-out insubordination. (The army's unofficial motto had by then become "don't mean nothin'," usually muttered sotto voce at the back of some annoying superior.)

On January 27, 1971, Private First Class James D. Moyler, a twenty-year-old helicopter crewman from Chesapeake, Virginia, carried matters further. After exchanging words over allegations of barracks theft, the black soldier flipped the safety off his M16 and in broad daylight shot C Troop's white commander at point-blank range. Captain Reichert bled to death in front of his own orderly room.

With the military justice system promptly cranking into high gear, Moyler was quickly arrested, jailed, charged, court-martialed, convicted, and sentenced to a long prison term. In the blink of an eye, he disappeared. From an institutional perspective, so too did the entire episode. In Saigon and Washington, those presiding over the war had no intention of allowing the death of Captain Reichert to affect their plans.

So in its sole report on the incident, the Pacific edition of *Stars and Stripes* offered the barest recitation of the facts—a masterful exercise in journalistic minimalism. As if in passing, however, the newspaper hinted at a larger context. Earlier that same month in Quang Tri Province, *Stripes* noted, one officer had been killed and another wounded "following a quarrel with enlisted men." Meanwhile, at Tan Son Nhut Air Base outside Saigon, someone had rolled a fragmentation grenade into the quarters of a military police officer, wounding him as he slept. Again, enlisted soldiers were suspected of perpetrating the attack, "although no one ha[d] been charged."[2]

In other words, what had occurred at An Khe, however shocking, did not qualify as particularly unusual. Disgruntled soldiers obliged to fight a war in which they (along with most of the country) had ceased to believe were not without recourse. Among the options available was the one PFC Moyler had chosen, turning weapons intended for use against the enemy on those whose authority they no longer recognized.

The implications of Moyler's action were, in military terms, beyond alarming. To sustain a massively unpopular war, the state had resorted to coercive means: report for duty or go to jail. At home, clever young men had become adept at evading that choice and so the war itself. Those less clever or more compliant ended up in uniform and in Vietnam. There, the nominally willing—now armed—were having second thoughts. In increasing numbers, they not only refused to comply but were engaging in acts of resistance.

The problem was Vietnam, of course. But the war had become inextricably tied to conscription. To save itself, the army desperately needed to free itself of the war—and of those compelled to serve against their will. Allowed to spread unchecked, the poisons made manifest at An Khe posed an existential threat to the institution as a whole. Even to a subaltern as callow and obtuse as I was, that much was apparent.

That other, unforeseen consequences might also ensue, unfavorable to the army, to soldiers, and to the country, did not occur to me. All that mattered then was to escape from an unendurable predicament. If that meant putting some distance between the army and the American people, so be it.

In the years that followed, the army effected that escape, shedding the war, the draft, and the tradition of a citizen-based military. Henceforth, the nation would rely on an all-volunteer force, the basis for a military system designed to preclude the recurrence of anything remotely resembling Vietnam ever again. For a time, Americans persuaded themselves that this professional military was a genuine bargain. Providing fighting forces of unrivaled capabilities, it seemingly offered assured, affordable security. It imposed few burdens. It posed no dangers.

In relieving ordinary citizens of any obligation to contribute to the country's defense, the arrangement also served, for a time at least, the interests of the military itself. In the eyes of their countrymen, those choosing to serve came to enjoy respect and high regard. Respect translated into generous support. Among the nation's budgetary priorities, the troops came first. Whatever the Pentagon said they needed, Washington made sure they got.

As a consequence, the army that I left in the early 1990s bore no more resemblance to the one into which I had been commissioned than a late model Ferrari might to a rusted-out Model T. The soldiers wanted to soldier. NCOs knew how to lead, and smart officers allowed them to do so. Given such a plethora of talent, even a mediocre commander could look good. As for an unofficial motto, the members of this self-consciously professional army were inexplicably given to shouting "Hooah" in chorus, exuding a confidence that went beyond cockiness.

Here, it appeared, was a win-win proposition. That the all-volunteer force was good for the country and equally good for those charged with responsibility for the country's defense seemed self-evident. Through the twilight years of the Cold War and in its immediate aftermath, I myself subscribed to that view.

Yet appearances deceived, or at least told only half the story. Arrangements that proved suitable as long as deterring the Soviet threat remained the U.S. military's principal mission and memories of jungles and rice paddies stayed fresh proved much less so once the Soviet empire collapsed and the lessons of Operation Desert Storm displaced the lessons of Vietnam. With change came new ambitions and expectations.

For a democracy committed to being a great military power, its leaders professing to believe that war can serve transcendent purposes, the allocation of responsibility for war qualifies as a matter of profound importance. Properly directed—on this, President George W. Bush entertained not the least doubt—a great army enables a great democracy to fulfill its ultimate mission. "Every nation," he declared in 2003, "has learned an important lesson," one that events since 9/11 had driven home. "Freedom is worth fighting for, dying for, and standing for—and the advance of freedom leads to peace."[3] Yet the phrasing of Bush's formulation, binding together war, peace, and freedom, might have left a careful listener wondering: *Who* fights? *Who* dies? *Who* stands? The answers to this triad of questions impart to democracy much of its substantive meaning.[4]

In the wake of Vietnam, seeking to put that catastrophic war behind them, the American people had devised (or accepted) a single crisp answer for all three questions: *not us*. Except as spectators, Americans abrogated any further responsibility for war in all of its aspects. With the people opting out, war became the exclusive province of the state. Washington could do what it wanted— and it did.

In the wake of 9/11, as America's self-described warriors embarked upon what U.S. leaders referred to as a Global War on Terrorism, the bills came due. A civil-military relationship founded on the principle that a few fight while the rest watch turned out to be a lose-lose proposition—bad for the country and worse yet for the military itself.

Rather than offering an antidote to problems, the military system centered on the all-volunteer force bred and exacerbated them. It underwrote recklessness in the formulation of policy and thereby resulted in needless, costly, and ill-managed wars. At home, the perpetuation of this system violated simple standards of fairness and undermined authentic democratic practice.

The way a nation wages war—the role allotted to the people in defending the country and the purposes for which it fights— testifies to the actual character of its political system. Designed to serve as an instrument of global interventionism (or imperial policing), America's professional army has proven to be astonishingly durable, if also astonishingly expensive. Yet when dispatched to Iraq and Afghanistan, it has proven incapable of winning. With victory beyond reach, the ostensible imperatives of U.S. security have consigned the nation's warrior elite to something akin to perpetual war.

Confronted with this fact, Americans shrug. Anyone teaching on a college campus today has experienced this firsthand: for the rising generation of citizens, war has become the new normal, a fact they accept as readily as they accept instruction in how to position themselves for admission to law school.

The approach this nation has taken to waging war since Vietnam (absolving the people from meaningful involvement), along with the way it organizes its army (relying on professionals), has altered the relationship between the military and society in ways that too few Americans seem willing to acknowledge. Since 9/11, that relationship has been heavy on symbolism and light on substance, with assurances of admiration for soldiers displacing serious consideration of what they are sent to do or what consequences ensue. In all the ways that actually matter, that relationship has almost ceased to exist.

From pulpit and podium, at concerts and sporting events, expressions of warmth and affection shower down on the troops. Yet when those wielding power in Washington subject soldiers to serial abuse, Americans acquiesce. When the state heedlessly and callously exploits those same troops, the people avert their gaze. Maintaining a pretense of caring about soldiers, state and society actually collaborate in betraying them.

This book subjects the present-day American military system to critical examination. It explains just how we got into the mess we're in. It shows who benefits and who suffers as a consequence. By way of remedy, it proposes that defending the country once more become a collective responsibility, inherent in citizenship.

PART I

NATION AT WAR

How war, which once served to enhance
American power and wealth,
became a source of national rack and ruin.

1

PEOPLE'S WAR

War is an unvarnished evil. Yet as with other evils—fires that clear out forest undergrowth, floods that replenish soil nutrients— war's legacy can include elements that may partially compensate (or at least appear to compensate) for the havoc inflicted and incurred.

For the United States, the Civil War offered one such occasion. To preserve the Union and destroy slavery, Americans served and sacrificed without stint. The citizen-soldiers who responded to the charge contained in the "Battle Hymn of the Republic"—"As He died to make men holy, let us die to make men free"—won a great victory. In doing so, they set the stage for the nation's emergence in the latter part of the nineteenth century as the world's preeminent economic power. Out of blood came muscle.

World War II proved to be a second such occasion for acquiring muscle, if not for other powers at least for the United States. Yet by 1941, in return for service and sacrifice, Americans expected rewards more tangible than the satisfaction of doing God's will. Once again, citizen-soldiers would fight for freedom. Thanks to the New Deal, however, freedom meant something more than submission to market forces. It now implied some measure of reciprocity, with citizens guaranteed access to the minimum essentials of life.

In describing what was at stake in World War II, President Franklin D. Roosevelt called this "freedom from want."[1] Making freedom thus defined available to the average American was by now becoming the job of political authorities in Washington. So in their approach to justifying war against the Axis, Roosevelt and his lieutenants shrewdly emphasized a shimmering consumer-oriented vision of democratic purpose.

To a greater extent than any prior conflict, mobilizing for World War II became an indisputably communal undertaking, involving quite literally everyone. So, too, did the war's actual conduct. As a result, the historian William O'Neill writes, the United States fought World War II as a "people's war." Rather than "uphold[ing] personal gratification as the be all and end all of life," Americans demonstrated a hitherto hidden capacity for government-prescribed collective action.[2] The appetite for personal gratification did not disappear. Yet at least for the duration Americans proved willing to curb it.

In this regard, the cultural moment was propitious. For a short time, the distance separating elite, middlebrow, and popular artistic expression seemed to collapse. Proletarian impulses released by the Great Depression persisted into the war years, infused now with a sense of hope that the promise of American life might indeed find fulfillment—and soon. Yearning and expectation gradually displaced the anger and despair that had characterized the 1930s. On symphony stages, this popular mood found expression in works like Aaron Copland's *Fanfare for the Common Man* (1942) and *Appalachian Spring* (1944). On Broadway, there was *Oklahoma!* (1943) by Richard Rodgers and Oscar Hammerstein.

("We know we belong to the land, and the land we belong to is grand!") At the movies, Oscar-nominated films such as *Mr. Smith Goes to Washington* (1939), *Our Town* (1940), *The Grapes of Wrath* (1940), and *Sergeant York* (1941) all mined the rich vein of populism. In photography these tendencies suffused the social realism of Dorothea Lange and Walker Evans. In painting, American regionalists such as Thomas Hart Benton, Grant Wood, and John Steuart Curry paid homage to ordinary workers while expressing nostalgia for small-town and rural America. In a war-specific context, there was the memorable work of the cartoonist Bill Mauldin, creator of the "dogface" soldiers Willie and Joe. Elitism had not disappeared from the American scene, but for a time it was thrown on the defensive.

"In a democracy," Undersecretary of War Robert Patterson declared in 1944, "all citizens have equal rights and equal obligations." A graduate of Harvard Law School, Patterson was himself a combat veteran of World War I. "When the nation is in peril," he continued, "the obligation of saving it should be shared by all, not foisted on a small percentage."[3] With regard to obligations (if not rights), Patterson's Axiom accurately described the Roosevelt administration's approach to war. All would contribute to the cause. All would share in whatever burdens the war effort imposed. All (or mostly all) could expect to share in the benefits, the president himself promising "jobs for those who can work. Security for those who need it. The ending of special privilege for the few. The preservation of civil liberties for all."[4]

At least as important was this unspoken caveat: although achieving victory would require shared sacrifice, the president would seek to limit the pain and suffering that Americans would actually endure. The price of defeating the Axis promised to be high. Yet FDR intended, wherever possible, to offload that price onto others, while claiming for the United States the lion's share of any benefits. For some (but not too much) pain, enormous gain—that describes the essence of U.S. grand strategy.

To an astonishing degree, Roosevelt and his lieutenants made good on both elements of this formula.

When it came to raising an army, therefore, inclusiveness became a defining precept. Rather than relying on volunteers, the United States implemented a system of conscription similar to the one devised for World War I. The draft took black and white, rich and poor, the famous and the obscure, Ivy Leaguers and high school dropouts. In order to field a force that peaked at twelve million serving members, the armed services inducted just about anyone meeting their mental and physical prerequisites. The sons of leading politicians like President Roosevelt served, as did the sons of multimillionaires like Joseph P. Kennedy. Hollywood idols Douglas Fairbanks Jr., Henry Fonda, Clark Gable, Tyrone Power, and James Stewart found themselves in uniform. So, too, did A-list movie directors Frank Capra, John Ford, John Huston, George Stevens, and William Wyler; baseball stars Ted Williams, Joe DiMaggio, and Hank Greenberg; and boxing greats Joe Louis and Gene Tunney.

In other words, the United States waged World War II with a citizen army that reflected the reigning precepts of American democracy (not least of all in its adherence to Jim Crow practices). Never again would U.S. forces reflect comparable diversity. Never again would they demonstrate comparable levels of overall effectiveness.

Service exacted sacrifice. Patterson's Axiom applied across the board. Among the four hundred thousand American lives claimed by World War II were nineteen players from the National Football League.[5] Glenn Miller, America's most popular bandleader, was killed while serving with the U.S. Army Air Forces. Harvard University contributed its share. Inscribed on one wall of the univer-

sity's Memorial Church are the names of 453 Harvard men who
died in World War II—just 35 fewer than the total number of West
Pointers lost.[6] Harvard's dead included four members of the university faculty and the nation's commander in chief (class of 1904).

The citizen-army's strengths and limitations as a fighting force
reflected—and affirmed—the civil-military contract forged for the
duration, the essence of which was a widely shared determination
"to get the goddam thing over and get home," the sooner the better.[7] According to the novelist James Gould Cozzens, a World War
II veteran, the average soldier lost little sleep contemplating the
question "why we fight." Only a single definition of purpose "carried or ever could carry any weight with him."

> His war aim was to get out as soon as possible and go home. This
> didn't mean that he wouldn't fight—on the contrary. Brought
> within fighting distance of the enemy, he saw well enough that
> until those people over there were all killed or frightened into
> quitting, he would never get home. He did not need to know
> about their bad acts and wicked principles. Compared to the
> offense they now committed . . . by shooting at him and keeping
> him here, any alleged atrocities of theirs, any evil schemes of
> their commanders, were mere trifles.[8]

Home signified homely satisfactions. "Your ordinary, plain,
garden-variety GI Joe," wrote Richard Polenberg in his popular
history of the war, "was fighting for the smell of fried chicken, or a
stack of Dinah Shore records on the phonograph, or the right to
throw pop bottles at the umpire at Ebbets Field."[9] Or as the journalist James Wechsler put it, throughout World War II, "the American soldier—happily—always remained a civilian. His vision of
the brave new world was hardly as luminous as that of editorial
writers. He wanted merely security and peace and a chance to go

back where he came from. . . . In a word, status quo ante, with trimmings."[10]

Such mundane aspirations did not imply a grant of authority allowing Roosevelt to expend American lives with abandon. Indeed, for FDR to assume otherwise would have placed his bargain with the American people at risk. Fortunately, circumstances did not require that the president do so. More fortunately still, he and his advisers understood that.

MACHINE WAR

The outcome of World War II turned, above all, on two factors: in Europe, the prowess and durability of the Red Army; in the Pacific, the weakness and vulnerability of the Japanese economy. To hit the perfect strategic sweet spot—winning big without losing too much—required the United States to exploit both of these factors. This Roosevelt ably succeeded in doing.

Success entailed making the most of America's comparative advantage in the production of war-essential matériel. Whatever the category—coal, oil, steel, foodstuffs, or finished goods like ships, tanks, and aircraft—no other belligerent could match the United States in productive capacity. Moreover, the American "arsenal of democracy"—difficult to attack and impossible to conquer—lay beyond the effective reach of Axis forces.[11] Not long after Pearl Harbor, the army chief of staff, General George C. Marshall, announced, "We are determined before the sun sets on this terrible struggle that our flag will be recognized throughout the world as a symbol of freedom on the one hand and of overwhelming power on the other."[12] Tapping that arsenal for all it was worth held the key to fulfilling Marshall's vision, which was also Roosevelt's.

The essential task was to expedite the conversion of U.S. economic might into Allied killing capacity. On that score, in the eyes of America's senior war managers, Soviet fighting power represented an asset of incalculable value. In Washington, Winston Churchill's speeches about the common heritage of the "English-speaking peoples," however inspiring, mattered less than did the Red Army's manifest ability to absorb and inflict punishment. "A democracy," Marshall later remarked, "cannot fight a Seven Years War."[13] When it came to waging total war, totalitarian dictatorships did not labor under comparable limitations. The people of the Soviet Union would fight as long as their supreme leader, Joseph Stalin, obliged them to do so.

With France defeated and the British empire short of will and wherewithal, the president looked to the Red Army to destroy the mighty *Wehrmacht*. "The whole question of whether we win or lose the war depends on the Russians," he told Treasury Secretary Henry Morgenthau in June 1942. That same year Admiral Ernest King, chief of naval operations, assured reporters in an off-the-record briefing that "Russia will do nine-tenths of the job of defeating Germany."[14]

Getting the Russians to shoulder the burden of defeating America's most dangerous adversary promised both to ensure support for the war effort on the home front and to position the United States to become victory's principal beneficiary. "The American people will not countenance a long war of attrition," the Pentagon's Joint War Plans Committee had warned in 1943.[15] A long war of attrition fought by the Soviet Union was altogether another matter, however. For Washington, providing Stalin with whatever the Soviet Union needed to stay in the fight (while easing any doubts the Soviet dictator might entertain about America's commitment to the cause) constituted not only a strategic priority but also a domestic political imperative.

To appreciate the implications of this arrangement—the Soviets doing most of the fighting while drawing freely on the endless bounty of American farms and factories—consider casualty statistics. At just above four hundred thousand, U.S. military deaths for the period 1941–45 were hardly trivial. Yet compared to the losses suffered by the other major belligerents, the United States emerged from the war largely unscathed. Estimates of Soviet battle losses, for example, range between eleven and thirteen million.[16] Add civilian deaths—ten million or more in the Soviet Union, a mere handful in the United States—and the disparity becomes that much greater. To ascribe this to the fortunes of war is to deny Roosevelt credit that is rightly his.

The U.S. approach to waging war against the Japanese empire offered a variation on the same theme. With opportunities for outsourcing that war less available (and less desired), the United States shouldered the principal responsibility for defeating a Japan that was as resource poor as the United States was resource rich. When it came to industrial capacity, Japan was a comparative pygmy, its economy approximately one-tenth as large as the American leviathan. In 1941, Japan accounted for 3.5 percent of global manufacturing output, the United States 32.5 percent. At the outset of hostilities, Japan was producing 5.8 million tons of steel and 53.7 million tons of coal annually. For the United States, the comparable figures were 28.8 million and 354.5 million.[17] As the war progressed, this gap only widened. The submarines that decimated Japan's merchant fleet and the bombers incinerating its cities brought the economy to its knees.

"In any week of her war with Germany between June 1941 and May 1945," writes the historian H. P. Willmott, succinctly expressing the genius of U.S. grand strategy, "the Soviet Union lost more dead than the total American fatalities in the Pacific war."[18] Many factors account for that disproportion, but among them were calculated choices made by FDR and his principal advisers: give the

Russians whatever they needed to kill and be killed fighting Germans; engage the *Wehrmacht* directly in large-scale ground combat only after it had been badly weakened; and fight the Japanese on terms that played to American advantages, expending matériel on a vast scale in order to husband lives.

"Our standard of living in peace," General Marshall had declared in September 1939, "is in reality the criterion of our ability to kill and destroy in war," adding that "present-day warfare is simply mass killing and mass destruction by means of machines resulting from mass production."[19] The unspoken corollary was this: the mass production of machines to wage war could enhance the American standard of living in the peace to follow. A preference for expending machines rather than men could—and did—produce strikingly positive effects on the home front.

Even today, the numbers remain startling. While a conflict of unprecedented scope and ferocity was devastating most of Eurasia, the United States enjoyed a sustained economic boom. Between 1939 and 1944, the nation's gross domestic product grew by 52 percent in constant dollars. Manufacturing output trebled. Despite rationing—inconvenience packaged as deprivation—consumer spending actually increased.[20]

More remarkable still, the benefits of this suddenly restored prosperity were broadly distributed. To be sure, the rich became richer, with the wartime pretax income of the top quintile of earners increasing by 55.7 percent. Yet the nonrich also benefited and disproportionately so. Families in the lowest quintile saw their incomes grow by 111.5 percent, in the second lowest by 116 percent.[21] Between 1939 and 1944, the share of wealth held by the richest 5 percent of Americans actually *fell*, from 23.7 percent to 16.8 percent.[22] The war that exhausted other belligerents and left untold millions in want around the world found Americans becoming not only wealthier but also more equal.

Notably, all of this happened despite (or because of) increased taxation. Throughout the war, tax policy remained a contentious issue. Overall, however, Americans paid more, and more Americans paid. Between 1940 and 1942, the corporate tax rate went from 24 to 40 percent, with an additional proviso taxing "excess" profits at 95 percent. Tax rates on individual income became more progressive even as larger numbers of wage earners were included in the system. In 1940, approximately 7 percent of Americans paid federal income taxes; by 1944, that figure had mushroomed to 64 percent. No one proposed that wartime might offer a suitable occasion for cutting taxes.[23]

None of this is to imply that World War II was a "good war," either on the fighting fronts or at home. If anything, the war stoked deep-seated prejudices and provided an outlet for modern-day pathologies. Race riots rocked major American cities. Bitter strikes paralyzed critical industries. Prostitution flourished. Unwanted pregnancies and sexually transmitted diseases proliferated. Social dislocation produced increases in juvenile delinquency. To this day, the mass incarceration of Japanese Americans remains a deeply embarrassing stain on President Roosevelt's record.

Yet if not good, Roosevelt's war was surely successful. If the essential objective of statecraft is to increase relative power, thereby enhancing a nation-state's ability to provide for the well-being of its citizens, then U.S. policy during World War II qualifies as nothing less than brilliant. Through cunning and foresight, he and his lieutenants secured for the United States a position of global preeminence while insulating the American people from the worst consequences of the worst war in history. If World War II did not deliver something for nothing, it did produce abundant rewards for much less than might have been expected.

Furthermore, the collaboration forged between government and governed yielded more than victory abroad. At home, it dramatically enhanced the standing of the former while reinvigorating the latter. The Great Depression had undermined the legitimacy of the American political system, prompting doubts about the viability of democratic capitalism. World War II restored that lost legitimacy with interest. As a people, Americans emerged from the war reassured that prosperity was indeed their birthright and eager to cash in on all that a fully restored American dream promised. Thanks to FDR's masterly handling of strategy, those gains came at a decidedly affordable price. War waged by the people had produced battlefield success and much more besides.

2

THE GREAT DECOUPLING

After September 11, 2001, when George W. Bush inaugurated the Global War on Terrorism, he saw another such victory ahead, one that would again refurbish and restore the nation's sense of purpose. "This time of adversity," the president declared in his 2002 State of the Union Address, "offers a unique moment of opportunity, a moment we must seize to change our culture." With the Afghan War seemingly all but won and an invasion of Iraq in the offing, Bush laid out his vision of renewal. "For too long," he lamented, "our culture has said, 'If it feels good, do it.'" No more, however. With the advent of global war, Americans were finding inspiration in heroic new role models, the president believed. The implications promised to be transformative. "Now America is embracing a new ethic and a new creed: 'Let's roll.' In the sacrifice of soldiers, the fierce brotherhood of firefighters, and the bravery and generosity of ordinary citizens, we have glimpsed what a new culture of responsibility could look like . . . a Nation that serves goals larger than self."

No such transformation ensued. Indeed, the way President

Bush chose to wage his war ensured a contrary result. If anything, the war on terror, stretching across more than a decade, served to mask a preexisting cultural crisis while setting the stage for large-scale economic calamity. In stark contrast to the Civil War and World War II, it depleted the nation's stores of moral capital, leaving in its wake cynicism and malaise along with chronic dysfunction. It impelled the country on a downward, not an upward, trajectory.

WHOSE WAR?

Embarking upon what he himself unfailingly described as an enterprise of vast historic significance, Bush wasted no time in excluding the American people from any real involvement. Choosing war, he governed as if there were no war.

"We have suffered great loss," the president acknowledged in a nationally televised address shortly after 9/11. "And in our grief and anger we have found our mission and our moment... The advance of human freedom... now depends on us. Our nation, this generation, will lift the dark threat of violence from our people and our future. We will rally the world to this cause by our efforts, by our courage. We will not tire, we will not falter and we will not fail."

But who exactly was this *we*? To whom was the president referring in his repeated and fervent use of the first-person plural?[1]

It soon became apparent that Bush's understanding of *we* differed substantially from Abraham Lincoln's "we here highly resolve" at Gettysburg. It differed more drastically still from FDR's in the post–Pearl Harbor declaration: "We are now in this war. We are all in it—all the way."[2]

Bush did not intend his *we* to be taken literally. It was nothing more than a rhetorical device, a vehicle for posturing. Minimizing collective inconvenience rather than requiring collective commitment became the distinctive signature of his approach to war management.

From the very outset, Bush made it clear that he wanted members of the public to carry on as before. After all, to suspend the pursuit of individual happiness (defined in practice as frantic consumption) was to hand the terrorists a "victory." So within three weeks of the 9/11 attacks, the president was urging his fellow citizens to "enjoy America's great destination spots. Get down to Disney World in Florida. Take your families and enjoy life, the way we want it to be enjoyed." To facilitate such excursions, the president persuaded Congress to cut taxes, a 2003 tax relief measure coming on top of one that he had already signed into law prior to 9/11.

In effect, George W. Bush inverted the stern inaugural charge issued by John F. Kennedy in 1961: "Ask not what your country can do for you." After 9/11, citizens had no need to ask. The Bush administration sought to anticipate their desires. To purchase support for or acquiescence in his global war (and the invasion and occupation of two countries in the Greater Middle East), the administration, with congressional approval, distributed bonuses at home.

Americans had little difficulty interpreting the president's prompts. In short order, the *we* called upon to advance the cause of human freedom took a backseat to the *we* called upon to enjoy life, whether in Disney World or elsewhere. Thus encouraged, Americans disengaged from Bush's war, leaving to others the task of waging it.

THE THREE NO'S

Senior military and civilian officials who managed World War II had viewed public support for the war effort as both critical and

finite, an essential asset to be carefully nurtured and no less carefully expended. Throughout the war years, concern that citizens
might balk at marching orders not to their liking remained omni-
present. Hence the pervasive propaganda aimed at sustaining
morale on the home front while painting a bright picture of all
that peace promised to bring in its wake. Hence, too, the determination of Pentagon planners to avoid asking of Americans more
than they were willing to give.

After 9/11, the Bush administration freed itself of any such
concerns. It did so by reformulating the allotted wartime role of
the public. "We're at war," President Bush told his vice president
on the morning of the attacks, and "someone's going to pay."[3]
What soon became clear was that the president's definition of
someone did not include the citizens of the United States.

In the immediate aftermath of 9/11, "United We Stand" held
sway as something akin to a national slogan, expressing shared
hurt, anger, and determination. Not for long, however. Within a
matter of months, although nominally "at war," the nation began
behaving as if it were "at peace." Americans had by then settled on
three first-person-plural axioms to describe the unofficial but invi-
olable parameters of their prospective wartime role.

- First, we will not change.
- Second, we will not pay.
- Third, we will not bleed.

According to the first postulate, Americans, heeding their
president, refused to permit war to exact demands. Instead, they
remained intent on pursuing their chosen conceptions of life, liberty, and happiness, unhindered and unencumbered. They would
accept no reordering of national priorities intended to facilitate
the war's prosecution.

According to the second postulate, Americans had no responsibility to cover the financial costs entailed by war's conduct. The
books need not balance. Increases in military expenditures, therefore, required neither increased revenue nor a willingness to accept
reduced services. Choosing between guns and butter was neither
necessary nor acceptable. To fund war, the government simply
borrowed.

According to the third postulate, actual participation in war
became entirely a matter of personal choice. Service (and therefore
sacrifice) was purely voluntary. War no longer imposed collective
civic duty—other than the necessity of signaling appreciation for
those choosing to serve.

As long as it abided by these proscriptions, Washington could
pretty much make war whenever, wherever, and however it wanted,
assured of at least tepid popular consent. In this decoupling of the
people from war waged in their name lay the Bush administration's most notable post-9/11 accomplishment. In place of a Lock-
ean social contract based on the concept of reciprocal responsibility,
a promissory note now provided the basis for waging war—and
the people who so casually endorsed that note had no expectation
of ever having to settle accounts.

As a consequence, war became exclusively the province of
the state rather than the country as a whole. Invited to indulge in
cheap grace, Americans willingly complied. Virtually from the outset, George W. Bush's Global War on Terrorism was never America's war in the sense that Lincoln's war and FDR's war had been.
It was—and at least in some quarters was intended to be—
Washington's war.

To appreciate this distinction, one need only note the gap
between the label Washington affixed to its war and the war's
actual conduct as it unfolded. To describe the conflict as a Global
War on Terrorism obfuscated existing realities. Neither global in

scope nor directed exclusively against terrorists, it was both far
less and much more than its name implied. According to President
Bush, the events of September 11, 2001, coming out of nowhere,
inaugurated the conflict. More accurately, the 9/11 attacks intensified a struggle that had been ongoing for decades. At issue most
immediately was the fate of a specific region: who would determine the future of the oil-rich, strategically critical Greater
Middle East? At issue in a broader sense were expectations, widely
entertained in Washington following the Cold War, of an ongoing
open-ended American Century—an extended period of unquestioned primacy exercised by the nation specifically charged with
charting history's course. In this sense, the stakes were not only
geopolitical but also teleological. Through war, Washington set
out after 9/11 to teach an object lesson to anyone tempted to challenge its writ. And through war, its reservoir of moral capital once
more filled to the brim, the United States would acquire the wherewithal to sustain a global Pax Americana into the distant future.
Such at least was the expectation.

Despite such lofty stakes, the conflict almost immediately
became and thereafter remained a third-person-plural enterprise:
they fought while *we* watched, uninvolved and seemingly unaf-
fected. The fighting *they* were American soldiers, members of an
institution that already existed at a considerable remove from
the rest of society. With something approaching unanimity,
ordinary citizens professed fervent admiration for these "warriors." Yet admiration did not imply mutual understanding, much
less intimacy. The actual relationship between soldiers and society
consisted for the most part of prayers offered at Sunday services,
pontificating by politicians of all stripes, and scripted rituals of
respect inserted into celebratory occasions like the Super Bowl or
the World Series.

In the corporate world, supporting the troops offered just one more way to sell product. "Here's to the heroes," Budweiser ad copy proclaimed. Depicting itself as "Proudly Serving Those Who Serve," the beer-making behemoth promised that for every home run hit during the 2011 major league baseball season it would donate one hundred dollars "to an organization that helps the families of fallen soldiers." This "Salute From the Stands" was something in which every fan could participate: "Please raise your Budweiser and join us in honoring those who keep our nation safe and free every Thirst Inning."[4]

Inviting those preferring Miller to Bud to "give a veteran a piece of the High Life," the Miller Brewing Company rolled out its own campaign to support the troops. "For every High Life cap or tab you drop off at participating retailers or mail in," the brewer promised to "donate 10¢ toward High Life Experiences for returning vets," including "sports events, concerts, outdoor adventures and more." For patriotic beer drinkers, it was a risk-free proposition: "Live the High Life. Give the High Life."[5]

So when it came to fighting and dying, not only did *we* get a free pass—we could feel good about it.[6] Courtesy of Bush administration tax policies, moreover, that free pass extended to defraying the war's financial costs. That obligation would fall on a second *they*—future generations of taxpayers, oblivious to the fate awaiting them.

Bush had inherited from his predecessor a balanced federal budget. After 9/11, increased military outlays combined with tax cuts drove that budget into the red. There it stayed. For fiscal year 2009, the year he left office, the federal deficit reached a staggering $1.4 trillion. Over the two terms of his presidency the size of the national debt more than doubled, ballooning from $3.3 trillion to $7.5 trillion. Worse still, the Bush administration's cavalier attitude toward budgetary orthodoxy—Vice President Dick Cheney announced that "deficits don't matter"—imparted to fiscal policy a momentum that proved exceedingly difficult to reverse.[7] Trillion-dollar annual shortfalls became routine.

Outsourcing war's conduct to a small warrior class—less than 1 percent of the total population—evoked occasional twinges of discomfort. Could such an approach to warfighting comport with authentic democratic principles? Obliging as-yet-unborn generations to foot the bill for wars in which they had no voice elicited similar expressions of concern. Were such arrangements consistent with the basic requirements of fairness? Such qualms of conscience did not produce action, however. No longer seeing war as an endeavor requiring collective effort on a national scale, adamant in refusing to curb their compulsion to consume, Americans swallowed hard, averted their gaze from the consequences of actions undertaken in their name, and did as President Bush bid them to do. So as war became permanent and perpetual, it also ceased to matter, at least as far as the great majority of Americans were concerned. Patterson's Axiom—the very concept of rights entailing obligations—had become a dead letter.

3

TALLYING UP

A post-9/11 approach to conducting war that found the country more or less AWOL while leaving the state free to do as it pleased ought to have set off alarms. Here was an arrangement rife with potential for moral and ethical mischief. Yet in politics, outcomes almost invariably matter more than issues of right and wrong. In evaluating the Global War on Terrorism, the overriding question is necessarily this one: has more than a decade of armed conflict enhanced the well-being of the American people? The wars fought by citizen-soldiers at the behest of Abraham Lincoln and Franklin Roosevelt did so. Can we say the same for the war launched by George W. Bush and perpetuated in modified form by Barack Obama?

Before taking stock of what a decade of war has actually produced, recall the expectations that prevailed shortly before war began. On the eve of the Civil War, optimism had given way to angst. After all, the country was in the process of coming apart. On the eve of World War II, the mood was similarly anxious. For a nation still caught in the throes of a protracted economic slump, the prospect of a European war carried limited appeal; the previous one, just two decades earlier, had yielded little but disappoint-ment. By comparison, expectations on the near side of the Global War on Terrorism were positively bullish. For citizens of the plan-et's "sole remaining superpower," the twentieth century had ended on a high note. The twenty-first century appeared rich with promise.

Speaking just prior to midnight on December 31, 1999, Presi-dent Bill Clinton surveyed the century just ending and identified its central theme as "the triumph of freedom and free people." To this "great story," Clinton told his listeners, the United States had made a pivotal contribution. Contemplating the future, he glimpsed even better days ahead—"the triumph of freedom wisely used." All that was needed to secure that triumph was for Ameri-cans to exploit and export "the economic benefits of globalization, the political benefits of democracy and human rights, [and] the educational and health benefits of all things modern." At the dawn-ing of the new millennium, he concluded confidently, "the sun will always rise on America as long as each new generation lights the fire of freedom."[1] What the president's remarks lacked in terms of insight or originality they made up for in familiarity. During the decade following the Cold War, such expectations had become commonplace. Skillful politician that he was, Clinton was telling Americans what they already believed.

The passing of one further decade during which U.S. forces seeking to ignite freedom's fire flooded the Greater Middle East reduced Bill Clinton's fin de siècle formula for peace and prosper-ity to tatters. In Iraq, Afghanistan, and Pakistan, the United States touched off a conflagration of sorts, albeit with results other than intended. Yet for the average American, the most painful setbacks occurred not out there in wartime theaters but back here on the home front. Instead of freedom wisely used, the decade's theme became: bubbles burst and dreams deflated.

Above all, those dreams had fostered expectations of unprecedented material abundance—more of everything for everyone. Alas, this was not to be. Although *crisis* ranks alongside *historic* atop any list of overused terms in American political discourse, the Great Recession that began in 2007 turned out to be the real deal: a crisis of historic proportions.

The titles of widely read books purporting to interpret that crisis told the tale. Stitched together, they offered a sorry narrative of a *Meltdown* attributed to *Reckless Endangerment* that plunged the economy into *Freefall*. For villains one needed to look no farther than Wall Street: *The Pirates of Manhattan* had *Hoodwinked* and fleeced an unwary public. *And Then the Roof Caved In,* as proponents of *Zombie Capitalism* engaged in *The Looting of America.* The nation's prosperity turned out to be built on A *House of Cards,* and government intervention proved ineffectual at best: *Bailout Nation* rescued the well-heeled but left plain folk to fend for themselves. The grim prospect of *Lost Decades* beckoned, perhaps even *The End of Growth* altogether. Americans who saw their wealth vanish never knew what hit them: straining to stay above water while foreigners got rich, they muttered *That Used to Be Us.* Featured prominently in the subtitles of these books were references to *hubris, greed, corruption, plunder,* and *wretched excess.*[2]

On this occasion at least, reality justified the hyperbole. With the ongoing "war" approaching the ten-year mark, the U.S. economy shed a total of 7.9 million jobs in just three years.[3] For only the second time since World War II, the official unemployment rate topped 10 percent. The retreat from that peak came at an achingly slow pace. By some estimates, actual unemployment—including those who had simply given up looking for work—was double the official figure.[4] Accentuating the pain was the duration of joblessness; those laid off during the Great Recession stayed out of work substantially longer than the unemployed during previous postwar economic downturns.[5] When new opportunities did eventually materialize, they usually came with smaller salaries and either reduced benefits or none at all.[6]

As an immediate consequence, millions of Americans lost their homes or found themselves "underwater," the value of their property less than what they owed on their mortgages. Countless more were thrown into poverty, the number of those officially classified as poor reaching the highest level since the Census Bureau began tracking such data.[7] A drop in median income erased gains made during the previous fifteen years.[8] Erstwhile members of the great American middle class shelved or abandoned outright carefully nurtured plans to educate their children or retire in modest comfort. Inequality reached gaping proportions with one percent of the population amassing a full 40 percent of the nation's wealth.[9]

Month after month, grim statistics provided fodder for commentators distributing blame and commiseration, for learned analysts offering contradictory explanations of why prosperity had proven so chimerical, and for politicians absolving themselves of responsibility while fingering as culprits members of the other party. Yet beyond its immediate impact, what did the Great Recession signify? Was the sudden appearance of hard times in the midst of war merely an epiphenomenon, a period of painful adjustment and belt-tightening after which the world's sole superpower would be back in the saddle? Or had the Great Recession begun a Great Recessional, with the United States in irreversible retreat from the apex of global dominion?

The political response to this economic calamity paid less attention to forecasting long-term implications than to fixing culpability. On the right, an angry Tea Party movement blamed Big Government. On the left, equally angry members of the Occupy movement blamed Big Business, especially Wall Street. What these two movements had in common was that each cast the American people as victims. Nefarious forces had gorged themselves at the expense of ordinary folk. By implication, the people were themselves absolved of responsibility for the catastrophe that had befallen them and their country.

Yet consider a third possibility. Perhaps the people were not victims but accessories. On the subject of war, Americans can no more claim innocence than they can regarding the effects of smoking or excessive drinking. As much as or more than Big Government or Big Business, popular attitudes toward war, combining detachment, neglect, and inattention, helped create the crisis in which the United States is mired.

THE TWO ONE-PERCENTS

A "country made by war," to cite the title of a popular account of U.S. military history, the United States in our own day is fast becoming a country undone by war.[10] Citizen armies had waged the wars that made the nation powerful (if not virtuous) and Americans rich (if not righteous). The character of those armies—preeminently the ones that preserved the Union and helped defeat Nazi Germany and Imperial Japan—testified to an implicit covenant between citizens and the state. According to its terms, war was the people's business and could not be otherwise. For the state to embark upon armed conflict of any magnitude required informed popular consent. Actual prosecution of any military campaign larger than a police action depended on the willingness of citizens in large numbers to become soldiers. Seeing war through to a conclusion hinged on the state's ability to sustain active popular support in the face of trial and adversity.

In their disgust over Vietnam, Americans withdrew from this arrangement. They disengaged from war, with few observers giving serious consideration to the implications of doing so. Events since, especially events since 9/11, have made those implications manifest. In the United States, war no longer qualifies in any meaningful sense as the people's business. In military matters, Americans have largely forfeited their say.

As a result, in formulating basic military policy and in deciding when and how to employ force, the state no longer requires the consent, direct participation, or ongoing support of citizens. As an immediate consequence, Washington's penchant for war has appreciably increased, without, however, any corresponding improvement in the ability of political and military leaders to conclude its wars either promptly or successfully. A further result, less appreciated but with even larger implications, has been to accelerate the erosion of the traditional concept of democratic citizenship.

In other words, the afflictions besetting the American way of life derive in some measure from shortcomings in the contemporary American way of war. The latter have either begotten or at least exacerbated the former.

Since 9/11, Americans have, in fact, refuted George C. Marshall by demonstrating a willingness to tolerate "a Seven Years [and longer] War." It turns out, as the neoconservative pundit Max Boot observed, that an absence of popular support "isn't necessarily fatal" for a flagging war effort. For an inveterate militarist like Boot, this comes as good news. "Public apathy," he argues, "presents a potential opportunity," making it possible to prolong "indefinitely" conflicts in which citizens are not invested.[11]

Yet such news is hardly good. Apathy toward war is symptomatic of advancing civic decay, finding expression in apathy toward the blight of child poverty,[12] homelessness,[13] illegitimacy,[14] and eating disorders[15] also plaguing the country. Shrugging off wars makes it that much easier for Americans—overweight,[16] overmedicated,[17] and deeply in hock[18]—to shrug off the persistence of widespread hunger,[19] the patent failures of their criminal justice system, and any number of other problems.[20] The thread that binds together this pattern of collective anomie is plain to see: unless the problem you're talking about affects me personally, why should I care?

For years after 9/11, America's armed forces floundered abroad. Although the invasions of Afghanistan and Iraq each began promisingly enough, in neither case were U.S. forces able to close the deal. With the fall of Richmond in April 1865, the Civil War drew to a definitive close. No such claim could be made in connection with the fall of Kabul in November 2001. When it came to dramatic effect, the staged April 2003 toppling of Saddam Hussein's statue in Baghdad's Firdos Square stands on a par with the September 1945 surrender ceremony on the deck of the USS *Missouri*. There, however, the comparison ends. The one event rang down the curtain; the other merely signified a script change. Meanwhile, Americans at home paid little more than lip service to the travails endured by the troops.

Beginning in 2007—just as the "surge" was ostensibly salvaging the Iraq War—a sea of troubles engulfed the home front. From those troubles, the continuation of war offered no escape. If anything, the perpetuation (and expansion) of armed conflict plunged the nation itself that much more deeply underwater. Once again, as in the 1860s and 1940s, war was playing a major role in determining the nation's destiny. Yet this time around, there was no upside.[21] Virtually all of the consequences—political, economic, social, cultural, and moral—proved negative. To a nation gearing up for global war, FDR had promised jobs, help for the vulnerable, an end to special privilege, the protection of civil liberties, and decisive military victory over the nation's enemies. To a considerable degree, Roosevelt made good on that promise. Judged by those same criteria, the Bush-Obama global war came up short on all counts.[22]

The crux of the problem lay with two symmetrical one-percents:

the 1 percent whose members get sent to fight seemingly endless wars and that other 1 percent whose members demonstrate such a knack for enriching themselves in "wartime." Needless to say, the two one-percents neither intersect nor overlap. Few of the very rich send their sons or daughters to fight. Few of those leaving the military's ranks find their way into the ranks of the plutocracy. Rather than rallying to the colors, Harvard graduates these days flock to Wall Street or the lucrative world of consulting.[23] Movie star heroics occur exclusively on-screen, while millionaire professional athletes manage to satisfy their appetite for combat on the court and the playing field.[24]

Yet a people who permit war to be waged in their name while offloading onto a tiny minority responsibility for its actual conduct have no cause to complain about an equally small minority milking the system for all it's worth. Crudely put, if the very rich are engaged in ruthlessly exploiting the 99 percent who are not, their actions are analogous to that of American society as a whole in its treatment of soldiers: the 99 percent who do not serve in uniform just as ruthlessly exploit the 1 percent who do.[25]

To excuse or justify their conduct, the very rich engage in acts of philanthropy. With a similar aim, the not-so-rich proclaim their undying admiration for the troops.

As the bumper sticker proclaims, freedom isn't free. Conditioned to believe that the exercise of global leadership is essential to preserving their freedom, and further conditioned to believe that leadership best expresses itself in the wielding of military might, Americans have begun to discover that trusting in the present-day American way of war to preserve the present-day American way of life entails exorbitant and unexpected costs.

Yet as painful as they may be, these costs represent something far more disturbing. As a remedy for all the ailments afflicting the body politic, war—at least as Americans have chosen to wage it—turns out to be a fundamentally inappropriate prescription. Rather than restoring the patient to health, war (as currently practiced pursuant to freedom as currently defined) constitutes a form of prolonged ritual suicide. Rather than building muscle, it corrupts and putrefies.

The choice Americans face today ends up being as straightforward as it is stark. If they believe war essential to preserving their freedom, it's incumbent upon them to prosecute war with the same seriousness their forebears demonstrated in the 1940s. Washington's war would then truly become America's war with all that implies in terms of commitment and priorities. Should Americans decide, on the other hand, that freedom as presently defined is not worth the sacrifices entailed by real war, it becomes incumbent upon them to revise their understanding of freedom. Either choice—real war or an alternative conception of freedom—would entail a more robust definition of what it means to be a citizen.

Yet the dilemma just described may be more theoretical than real. Without the players fully understanding the stakes, the die has already been cast. Having forfeited responsibility for war's design and conduct, the American people may find that Washington considers that grant of authority irrevocable. The state now owns war, with the country consigned to observer status. Meanwhile, the juggernaut of mainstream, commercial culture continues to promulgate the four pop Gospels of American Freedom: novelty, autonomy, celebrity, and consumption. Efforts to resist or reverse these tendencies, whether by right-leaning traditionalists (many of them religiously inclined) or left-leaning secular humanists (sometimes allied with religious radicals) have been feeble and ineffective.

Americans must therefore accept the likelihood of a future in which real if futile sacrifices exacted from the few who fight will serve chiefly to facilitate metaphorical death for the rest who do not.

PART II

WARRIOR'S PLIGHT

*How America's army after Vietnam, seeking
reconciliation and relevance, became isolated from
society and mired in unwinnable wars.*

4

AMERICA'S ARMY

From the founding of the Republic to the present moment, debates over U.S. military policy have turned on two enduring questions: What is the nature and purpose of the American army? Where does the ordinary soldier stand in relation to American society?

Of course, along with its army, the United States possesses a formidable navy, proudly tracing its origins back to the Revolution. Since 1947, the nation has also maintained a powerful independent air force. Then there is the U.S. Marine Corps, an adjunct of the navy that is a second army of sorts and possesses its own air force.

When it comes to stature, America's army ranks as the least among these several services. Since World War II, no competitor has come even close to challenging U.S. naval supremacy. The same applies to airpower; the U.S. Air Force defines the gold standard and has done so since the day of its establishment. As for the marines, quite apart from their reputation as redoubtable fighters, the Corps has acquired an aura of its own. In American culture and public esteem, marines—deservedly—occupy a special niche.

If America's army occupies a niche, it's that of the redheaded stepchild. Rarely has that service inspired genuine warmth or affection. Its institutional persona is Olive Drab—flat, bland, and dull. In a country where appearance means everything, the army is glamour-challenged. It seldom generates buzz. It lacks pizzazz. On the sex appeal meter, it barely moves the needle. Try as it might to devise a fashionable image, it defines the inverse of hip.

Yet to a greater extent than any other national institution— more than the other armed services, more than any branch of the federal government, more perhaps than Hollywood or Wall Street—the army and the soldiers filling its ranks testify to the essence of American democracy. Who serves and on what basis? To answer those questions is to lay bare the prevailing conception of citizenship. Similarly, the uses to which policy makers put the army serve as a barometer of how the United States addresses the world beyond its borders. When it comes to foreign policy, what Washington says matters much less than where its soldiers go (or don't go), as well as what they do (and don't do) upon arrival. In short, the army's organization and its functions disclose in a tangible way what Americans actually value and what the United States actually stands for.

Since its founding, the army's character has changed dramatically, never more so than in our own time. Back in 1775, "embattled farmers"—an armed citizenry fighting for national independence—defined its essence.[1] In today's army, "warriors" fill the ranks of a thoroughly professionalized force. During the century and a half in which the United States completed the journey from modest-sized republic to global superpower, the army had straddled two competing traditions. On the one hand was the citizen-soldier, successor to the "embattled farmer," who in time of need rallied to the colors and won big wars. On the other was the long-service regular, precursor to today's warrior elite, who in the intervals between big wars fought small ones while enforcing America's writ throughout an ever-expanding imperium.

In the 1840s, citizen-volunteers invaded Mexico and seized California. Subsequently, they saved the Union and ended slavery. At the end of the nineteenth century, they put paid to Spain's crumbling empire in the Caribbean and across the Pacific. In one world war, citizen-conscripts played a role in toppling the Kaiser; in a second, they helped defeat the Führer, Il Duce, and the god-emperor of Imperial Japan. The soldiers who claimed these achievements traced their heritage to Lexington, Concord, and Bunker Hill. If the worth of the causes for which they fought varied, the army whose ranks they filled remained thoroughly, even raucously democratic.

Meanwhile, with much less fanfare, regulars labored to "tame" the American West. After 1898, they pacified the Philippines, helped suppress the Boxer Rebellion, and generally made themselves useful manning outposts of empire that the United States accumulated from Havana to Tientsin. The army in which they served advanced America's purposes while winning little popular acclaim or gratitude. Rather than spreading democracy abroad, soldiers clad in blue and then in khaki enhanced the power and dominion of the United States, which over time facilitated the establishment of something approximating genuine democracy at home.

After World War II, maintaining this neat division of labor— one type of army responsible for the occasional ideologically charged crusade while a second handled the imperatives of imperial policing during the nominally peaceful intervals between— was no longer possible. After 1945, the era of really big wars came to a close (or at least entered an extended pause). With the advent of nuclear weapons, *total war* became a theoretical construct, supplanted by *limited war*, also a theoretical construct but one devised to describe actually existing events. America's Cold War army never fought the Soviet enemy, said to pose an existential threat and therefore requiring an all-out effort. The enemies that the army did fight never even approximated existential threats. Wars of policy rather than wars of survival, these conflicts merited a less than all-out effort, and that's what they got.

The postwar wars occurred on a scale too small to elicit a sustained, full-fledged national commitment, yet too large for a prewar-style regular army to handle. Although American soldiers in 1950 were fighting the Chinese much as they had done in 1900, there was no mistaking the Korean War for the Boxer Rebellion. The criticism heaped on President Harry S. Truman's head when he foolishly referred to Korea as a *police action* makes the point. The intervention that suppressed the Boxers *had been* a police action of sorts. To apply that term to combat on the scale occurring in Korea seemed somehow obscene.

In short, national security requirements after 1945 made the army's dual tradition unsustainable. With the world seemingly teetering on the precipice of nuclear cataclysm, the nation could no longer rely on a small regular army for everyday needs while mobilizing a much larger citizen-army in times of great emergency. Emergency had become an everyday condition. In an effort to amalgamate elements of both traditions, civilian and military leaders sought to create in what was nominally peacetime an army that possessed considerable fighting power, could be relied upon to do the bidding of the state, and still retained links to American society.

The result, forged in Korea and reaching maturity in the early 1960s, was a large citizen-soldier army designed for the ostensible purpose of keeping the Cold War cold, yet providing a formidable force-in-being available for commitment wherever that war showed signs of turning hot. The mechanism employed to sustain this army while retaining some semblance of a democratic gloss was the "peacetime" draft.

F. T. A.

This was the army that in 1965 deployed to Vietnam, where it met with catastrophic failure. How exactly to apportion responsibility for that failure remains the subject of dispute. With plenty of blame to go around, civilian leaders like President Lyndon Johnson and Secretary of Defense Robert McNamara have come in for their fair share. So, too, have military leaders, some prominent like General William Westmoreland (symbolizing ineptitude), others obscure like Lieutenant William Calley (symbolizing criminality). Yet the media (said to be biased), antiwar protesters (said to be cowardly), the Congress (said to be craven), and the South Vietnamese (in American eyes, corrupt and indolent) have not escaped unscathed.

Regardless of where the fault lay, the impact of failure visited upon the American army was indisputable: under the stress of protracted, inconclusive war, it all but collapsed. By the early 1970s, the army had ceased to be an effective fighting force and resembled something akin to a demoralized, violence-prone rabble.[2]

Contemplating the army that dragged itself out of Vietnam, a sympathetic observer described it as besieged "from without and within by social turbulence, pandemic drug addiction, race war, sedition, civilian scapegoatism, draftee recalcitrance, barracks theft and common crime, all but abandoned by government, by Congress, and by the public it thought it was defending." The result was an institution "battered by a crisis of discipline, lowered self-esteem, and negative morale unlike anything ever found in its past experience."[3] In the eyes of many Americans—especially the young—that army now represented the very *antithesis* of democracy. Rather than eliciting popular empathy and support, soldiers became—or at least believed they had become—the target of obloquy.[4]

As a consequence of Vietnam and the upheaval of the 1960s, the army had fallen radically out of step with American society. However much members of Richard Nixon's "silent majority" might resent the proliferation of antiwar, antimilitary, antiestablishment attitudes—a resentment that Nixon skillfully tapped to win the White House—they did not define the temper of the times. Activists, radicals, and hipsters celebrating a do-your-own-thing spontaneity drove the culture. In their eyes, the army appeared cold, impersonal, repressive, and bureaucratic—an environment where "stockade brutality and drumhead courts-martial" awaited anyone disinclined to conform.[5] That such an institution might advance the cause of anyone's liberation anywhere was patently preposterous. By its very nature, it denied freedom, enforced conformity, and demanded submission. In short, the army was to the members of the countercultural left what abortion would soon become for the religious right: the preeminent symbol of all they despised.

The feeling was mutual. "Society's distrust of soldiers," wrote the journalist Ward Just in 1970, "is equaled only by the distrust of soldiers for society." Among officers, he continued, "the sense of isolation was palpable."[6] The regular army had always resented the lack of warmth and appreciation it received from the general public. For members of the officer corps, a sense of alienation and victimization now became acute. As one highly decorated soldier put it, "We're the scapegoat for Vietnam."[7]

Worse still, the army proved unable to insulate itself from the turmoil engulfing the home front. Counterinsurgency abroad found its counterpart in insurgency within. Much to the distress of senior military leaders, antiwar, antimilitary, and antiestablishment attitudes infiltrated the army's ranks.[8] At a time when every-thing from hair and music to sex had become intensely politicized, the army found itself a political battleground of sorts.[9] Under-ground newspapers staffed by self-described radicals sought to subvert what remained of the service's internal order and disci-pline.[10] Antiwar GI "coffeehouses" located outside the gates of major bases sowed seeds of dissent. On the graffiti-scarred walls of barracks or latrines, F. T. A. (Fuck the Army) became as omnipres-ent as KILROY WAS HERE had been in an earlier day. Incidents of collective insubordination proliferated.[11] A contest to win the "hearts and minds" of the rank and file ensued, with senior offi-cers fearing that they might achieve no more success than they had in Vietnam. The army, Ward Just wrote at the time, "does not know how to contain the revolution."[12]

Concerned members of Congress took note. South Carolina Republican Senator Strom Thurmond convened hearings to inves-tigate "revolutionary organizations" engaged in a "systematic effort to spread disaffection in our armed forces and to cause insubordi-nation, disloyalty, mutiny, or refusal of duty." One government investigator summoned to testify charged that a "cadre of civilian activists dedicated to the weakening of the military as a step toward the ultimate overthrow of the U.S. Government" was targeting enlisted members of the military. "Their goal is the violent destruc-tion of U.S. society." Among the organizations cited were the Cen-ter for Servicemen's Rights, the Movement for a Democratic Military, the Black Military Resistance League, the Fort Bragg GI Union, and Vietnam Veterans Against the War.[13]

Vietnam itself became the incubator of revolutionary action. From there, for example, the practice of intimidating or assassinat-ing unpopular leaders (*fragging*) emerged.[14] Yet Vietnam-induced pathologies soon permeated the entire army. In Europe, where a quarter of a million American soldiers ostensibly stood ready to fend off a Warsaw Pact attack, the rot was widespread. There, endemic race violence beset the U.S. Seventh Army.[15] Drug use was commonplace.[16]

In 1970, *Look* magazine dispatched a reporter and photographer to take the temperature of the crack regiment assigned to defend the famous Fulda Gap. The conditions they found were more than slightly troubling. GIs flashed peace signs as "the newest salute" and professed to find it unnecessary "to go out and point the big guns at the other side." Throughout the unit, the racial climate was toxic. Referring to themselves as "soul brothers," African American enlisted troopers were, according to *Look,* as "tight as fists," the metaphor suggesting both solidarity and pent-up resentment. Small-scale disputes between blacks and whites had a way of escalating into quasi–race riots. When the befuddled white regimental commander "authorized black culture classes during duty hours" as a way of defusing anger, he was accused of appeasing malcontents. Meanwhile, rumors of a regimental KKK klavern organized by white noncoms drew official attention. Illegal drug use was rampant. "People don't drink on duty," *Look* quoted one unnamed officer as saying. "People damn well smoke pot on duty." The professionals didn't know how to handle soldiers the magazine candidly described as "militants." Here was a leadership challenge for which army field manuals provided no ready answer. "We're making these desperate efforts to communicate with them," one officer remarked, referring to the soldiers in the ranks. The efforts weren't working.[17]

Complicating the challenge of containing that revolution was the fact that it was so difficult to define. It was sex, drugs, and rock and roll. It was race, class, and gender. The revolution to which army dissidents professed loyalty offered liberation from received traditions and sources of authority, while demanding conformity with newly invented dogmas. Senior officers accustomed to being in charge intensely disliked demands for self-actualization coming from the bottom up.

Of course, venting, of which there was plenty, did not necessarily translate into programs of effective political action. The overwrought fears of Senate investigators notwithstanding, soldier-radicals posed no direct threat to the established political order. Even so, for those accustomed to receiving unquestioned obedience, GI dissidents represented a subversive presence, importing into the ranks values and attitudes to which their contemporaries "on the outside" had now sworn allegiance. Soldier-dissidents also mirrored their civilian counterparts in their tendency to strike angry poses and to lump their complaints into one massive undifferentiated indictment. So in the Seventh Army, the newsletter of a soldier organization called FighT bAck could announce its opposition to "imperialist wars such as Indochina," to "racism and discrimination against women," to the military "being used as scab labor to break strikes," and to national security policies designed to suit "huge American corporations and banks, [but] not in the interest of the American people."[18] How exactly FighT bAck intended to correct these injustices was not at all clear. Yet the very existence of such organizations and the defiance they expressed induced concern bordering on panic among senior military leaders. For the brass, the challenges posed by the Vietcong and the People's Army of Vietnam paled in comparison.

As a consequence of the Vietnam War, the army found itself face-to-face with two mutually reinforcing crises, one internal and one external. Internally, it confronted a crisis of authority, being no longer able to assert discipline and command subservience. Externally, it faced a crisis of legitimacy as an institution no longer able to elicit respect and induce popular support, especially among the young. The foremost symbol of both crises was the draft. As a first step toward restoring authority and legitimacy, eliminating conscription came to seem an imperative. Yet however essential, this negative step alone could not suffice. There could be no real restoration—no reopening of lines of "communication" with soldiers and the American people—without some degree of accommodation.

DICK'S TRICK

By the time Richard Nixon reclaimed center stage in American politics amid the serial detonations of 1968, questions regarding the army's nature and purpose along with the ordinary soldier's relationship to American society had acquired unusual urgency. The "issue of army service," writes the historian Beth Bailey, served as a proxy "for some of the most important issues of the age." When citizens and politicians directed their ire toward (or expressed support for) the army, they were actually arguing "over who belongs in America and on what terms, over the meaning of citizenship and the rights and obligations it carries, over whether equality or liberty is the more central of American values, and over what role the military should play in the United States, not only in times of war, but in times of peace."[19]

Nixon himself had no more than a peripheral interest in such lofty concerns. What mattered to him was power: gaining it, preserving it, and using it. As a presidential candidate, he had announced his own opposition to the draft, couching his argument in principled terms. "A system of compulsory service that arbitrarily selects some and not others simply cannot be squared with our whole concept of liberty, justice, and equality under law. . . . The only way to stop the inequities is to stop using the system. . . . I say it's time we looked to our consciences. Let's show our commitment to freedom by preparing to assure our young people theirs."[20]

Yet beneath the lofty sentiments was Nixonesque opportunism: promising to end the draft offered the prospect of peeling off some antiwar votes. Acting on that promise once elected by actually deep-sixing the draft just might induce foot soldiers in the antiwar movement to leave the streets and return to their classrooms, thereby allowing the new president greater latitude in formulating policy.

Soon after taking office, Nixon did follow through, convening a commission of wise men to evaluate the possibility of establishing an all-volunteer military. When that commission obligingly affirmed the feasibility of the president's wishes, he wasted no time in moving to terminate conscription.[21]

To a considerable degree, Nixon accurately gauged the effects of doing so. The antiwar movement did not disappear, but it lost steam. Americans as a whole greeted the end of the draft, one observer noted, with "a few boos, fewer cheers, and lots of apathy."[22] So although Nixon had run for the presidency vowing to end the Vietnam War, eliminating the draft permitted him instead to prolong it. Four full years later, with the war still in progress, he easily won election to a second term. Imagine Barack Obama, running for the White House in 2008 on the promise of ending the Iraq War, expanding it instead, and winning reelection in 2012 by a landslide. This describes Nixon's feat.

Promising to end conscription had helped Nixon win in 1968; fulfilling that promise had given him a freer hand to govern while contributing to political victory in 1972. For Nixon and his lieutenants, that's all that really mattered. In deciding to reformulate the character of the army and revise the relationship of soldier to society, the commander in chief acted in response to near-term political calculations. Long-term implications? Those were for others to worry about. Few did at the time. Someone like Joseph Califano, former White House aide to President Lyndon Johnson, might suggest that "by removing the middle class from even the threat of conscription, we remove perhaps the greatest inhibition on a President's decision to wage war."[23] Yet conscription hadn't dissuaded Harry Truman from intervening in Korea in 1950 or stopped Johnson from plunging into Vietnam in 1965, facts that sapped Califano's argument of its persuasive power.

Someone like General Westmoreland might cling to the view that "deeply embedded within the American ethos is the idea that every citizen is a soldier." Absent "the continuous movement of citizens in and out of the Service," the old general fretted that the army could "become a danger to our society—a danger which our forefathers so carefully tried to preclude." But Vietnam had destroyed whatever remained of that ethos along with whatever credibility the general himself may have once possessed. According to the historian Robert Griffith, other senior officers took a different view. "If the dissent, undiscipline, and drug and alcohol abuse were indeed imports from society, they reasoned, reduced reliance on the draft and unwilling draft-motivated volunteers might offer a way for the Army to solve some of its own social problems. In a smaller post-Vietnam Army of true volunteers, professional standards could be established and dissidents, malcontents, and misfits weeded out."[24]

Westy might wax nostalgic about "an army of the people . . . directed by the people" through their elected representatives.[25] But that army had ceased to exist. So, too, had those people. Reluctantly or not, most generals accepted that verdict.

GOOD-BYE CHICKENSHIT

Yet the termination of the draft left the army's leadership with a mountain of worry. How to induce sufficient numbers of smart, able-bodied young Americans to volunteer for military service posed a daunting challenge, made more so by the ongoing cultural upheaval to which the 1960s had given birth and by the fact that Vietnam itself remained the freshest of memories. After some initial missteps, the army performed creditably in rising to that challenge. It accommodated (at times grudgingly) the changing cultural landscape and successfully rebranded itself, transforming army service into a potential opportunity rather than a burdensome imposition.

Making the all-volunteer army work required not only inducing would-be recruits to enlist but also persuading serving soldiers to stay on for the long haul. Selling the army as a career required better pay and benefits, which Congress obligingly provided with a series of pay hikes that began in 1971. That year, for example, the base pay of a new recruit more than doubled from $134 to $288 per month. Freshly commissioned second lieutenants saw their monthly pay jump from $450 to $611 per month, not including benefits.[26]

Selling the army also entailed changing the day-to-day experience of military life. It meant doing away with the make-work that had traditionally formed such a large part of a soldier's daily routine and reducing what the literary critic Paul Fussell, recalling his own military service, had labeled *chickenshit*.[27]

Traditionally, the term *soldier*, especially when used as a verb, had implied the avoidance of work. *To soldier* meant to shirk, malinger, or feign illness—an entirely rational response to tasks that were demeaning, repetitious, and lacked evident purpose.[28] Service in the draft-era army had included plenty of all three: pulling weeds, painting rocks, and performing housekeeping chores like KP (Kitchen Police).[29] For unmarried soldiers, the draft-era army also implied austere living conditions, sleeping alongside others in open bays and sharing latrine facilities. Privacy was nonexistent, with personal possessions subject to inspection at the whim of anyone in authority.

In peacetime, the army had treated the draftee as an unskilled day laborer, available to perform whatever tasks might need doing. In the volunteer army, a soldier's time acquired value. An increasingly costly commodity, it was not to be wasted on nonessentials. Although a certain amount of make-work and chickenshit persisted, training—acquiring, demonstrating, and sustaining specific military skills—now became the centerpiece of soldierly existence. Scrubbing pots and pans, grooming the parade ground, and even guarding the front gate—these routine functions the army began contracting out to civilian firms, with implications that became evident only decades later. For once begun, this policy of privatization had no self-evident limit. Here was another insurgency of sorts, for-profit enterprises taking over turf the army had previously claimed as its own. In pursuit of economy, the army forfeited self-sufficiency.

Accompanying this conversion of the common soldier from poorly paid laborer to decently compensated specialist or aspiring professional were comparable changes in lifestyle. Draftees by and large had been single. Better paid and longer serving, volunteer soldiers demonstrated a propensity to marry, obliging the army to become "family friendly." For commanders, building and staffing child-care centers became a priority. So, too, did accommodating the aspirations of military spouses, no longer content to accept the designation of "dependent" while offering their services as volunteers, that is, unpaid auxiliaries.

Life for military families residing off-base became all but indistinguishable from the life of nonmilitary families living next door or down the street, even if Dad (or Mom) was in a somewhat unusual line of work. So, too, with those single soldiers residing on post. Rather than resembling confinement to a minimum-security prison, barracks life acquired some of the atmospherics of a college dorm. Army plans for housing the troops now touted "carpeted, air-conditioned townhouses, furnished in motel-modern plastic and veneer [and] nestled together with landscaped courtyards and lawns."[30] Both on duty and off, the army became a place that Beetle Bailey would have scarcely recognized and into which he would not have been allowed entry.

5

COMES THE REVOLUTION

Yet putting the volunteer army on a healthy footing required more than better pay and benefits, more rigorous training, and a more comfortable lifestyle. It entailed courting groups that demonstrated a particular propensity to enlist or had been notably underrepresented during the draft era. Prominent in the first category were African Americans. Prominent in the second were women.

In both cases, the key to courtship lay in removing barriers to opportunity. In post-Vietnam America, the operative definition of *equality* emphasized leveling the playing field. Yet even in the 1960s, when it came to participation, promotion, and access to power, the army clung to rules, written and unwritten, that favored white males. The viability of the all-volunteer force depended at least in part on the army's ability to create credible paths to career success for those who were not white and not male. "With the advent of the volunteer military," the sociologist Charles Moskos wrote nearly thirty years ago, "the white middle-class soldier became something of an endangered species."[1] Into the breach created by his departure came the black working-class soldier and women of all colors.

BLACK BOSSES

With regard to race, although the army had officially desegregated during the Korean War, equality was less than perfect. In the enlisted ranks, African American males did enjoy considerable upward mobility. Even during the draft era, the noncommissioned officer corps was disproportionately black. Yet access to commissioned ranks—still then carrying the connotation of "officer and gentleman"—remained restricted, especially at the senior levels.[2] So although Benjamin O. Davis Sr. had achieved the rank of brigadier general during World War II—his promotion an act of undisguised tokenism—it was a full twenty years *after* President Harry Truman ordered the armed services to integrate before the army had its second black general officer.[3]

A nation awash in pervasive racial discrimination, as was the United States even after World War II, found this entirely tolerable—indeed, could congratulate itself on the relatively generous opportunities granted the Negro in military service. By the beginning of the 1970s, however, with the draft ending, the army's this-far-but-no-farther approach to racial equality no longer sufficed. The battle to preserve legal segregation had ended in ignominious defeat. Where overt racism lingered, it had become the preserve of yahoos, louts, and the incorrigibly ignorant. Even southern senators found themselves obliged to adjust their attitudes—or at least to make a pretense of doing so.

Equally important, the rise of the Black Power movement signaled a new assertiveness among African Americans, especially notable among the very age groups the army was most eager to recruit. Counting on black volunteers to enlist in large numbers while keeping the officer corps almost entirely white was not a recipe that promised success. The circumscribed equality that had sufficed into the 1960s would no longer do. The racial disharmony roiling the army (as well as the other services) during the latter part of the Vietnam era—manifesting itself in widespread, ostentatious self-segregation and no small amount of violence—had made that obvious to all.[4] One thing was clear: the all-volunteer experiment was never going to get off the ground unless each of the armed services demonstrated an unambiguous commitment to creating a race-neutral force.

Whatever the proportions of institutional self-interest and enlightened consciousness involved, real change ensued in remarkably short order. The African American presence at the United States Military Academy offers an illustrative example. Even in the 1960s, the total number of blacks in any entering West Point class never exceeded ten, with African Americans during that decade constituting less than one percent of the Corps of Cadets.[5] My own West Point class, graduating a total of eight hundred cadets in 1969, included a grand total of eight African Americans.[6]

Prior to the 1960s, such underrepresentation elicited little notice. By the end of that decade, it had become a problem to which the academy leadership began to attend. The class entering West Point a month after I left included forty-four black cadets. Six years later, the class of 1979 had eighty-six African Americans, numbers thereafter fluctuating between eighty and one hundred per class. When Benjamin O. Davis Jr. received his diploma as a member of the class of 1936, he became the *first* black West Pointer of the twentieth century and only the *fourth* to graduate from the United States Military Academy since its founding in 1802. Yet by 1991, reflecting the army's post-Vietnam commitment to racial equality, the one thousandth black West Pointer had joined the Long Gray Line.[7]

Something similar was occurring in the senior ranks. In June 1971, the number of African American brigadier generals on active duty in the U.S. Army stood at zero. One year later there were three; a year later seven; by June 1974 ten. From 1980 to 2010, the number of African Americans serving as brigadier generals in the regular army averaged thirteen, only twice dropping below ten—even as the total inventory of army brigadier generals was falling by 40 percent due to post-Vietnam and post–Cold War personnel reductions.[8]

The point is not that the army banished every last taint of racism. Yet to the extent that the "revolution" associated with the 1960s had a racial dimension, the army adapted itself to its requirements with alacrity and effectiveness. As a consequence, by the 1990s it had become "the only place in America where blacks routinely boss around whites."[9]

GI JANE

With regard to gender, the army traveled a more circuitous route but arrived at nearly the same destination. In the aftermath of World War II, the Women's Armed Services Integration Act, signed into law in 1948, had established a niche for women in the peacetime military. Yet rather than "integrating" women in any meaningful sense, the legislation created a gendered version of "separate but equal." The law directed that no more than 2 percent of the total force be female. It established colonel (or, in the navy, captain) as the highest rank to which women could aspire—there would be no generals or admirals in skirts. It prohibited women from serving on warships or crewing combat aircraft, largely confining them to medical and administrative duties. By converting the Women's Army Corps from wartime expedient into permanent entity, the legislation guaranteed women the opportunity to serve—not a trivial achievement—but only as second-class citizen-soldiers.

These terms of reference persisted well into the 1960s when they began to give way, the demands of feminists converging with the imperatives of "manning" a postconscription army. One obvious way to ease the transition to an all-volunteer force was to remove the 2 percent cap on the number of women in uniform, effectively doubling the pool of potential volunteers. Yet an exclusively male army leadership keen to increase the number of women in the ranks had no intention of ceding its authority to dictate the parameters under which women would serve. Any cultural or ideological insistence on absolute gender equality would take a backseat to a professional weltanschauung that saw war as an essentially masculine domain. Such was the intent anyway.

Although generals and admirals did fight a determined rearguard action to preserve male primacy, their efforts proved largely (although not entirely) futile. As with race, so, too, with gender: proponents of social change seized upon military service as a realm in which to press their broader agenda, with gender traditionalists—now labeled sexists—thrown on the defensive. On the political correctness scale, the military's version of Jane Crow soon ranked only slightly above the now thoroughly discredited system of Jim Crow. By the 1970s, an army eager to recruit women in unprecedented numbers confronted a choice. It could abandon the proposition that war should remain a male preserve, endorsing gender equality as fully compatible with military effectiveness. Alternatively, it could *selectively* lift some limitations on women in military service, while maintaining actual combat as an exclusively male pursuit—knowing full well that women's rights advocates were unlikely to find such half measures acceptable.

The army leadership chose the latter course with predictable results. Those campaigning for women's rights adamantly refused to accept anything less than full equality. As a consequence, the army found itself obliged to cede yet more ground, which it did neither gracefully nor happily.

So whereas the post-Vietnam army had worked hard to increase the number of black cadets at West Point, it worked just as hard or harder to keep women out altogether. Since its founding, the United States Military Academy had been an all-male institution. With something close to unanimity, army leaders (and West Point alumni) favored that arrangement and saw no reason why the advent of the all-volunteer force should require change. As a very young officer, I myself subscribed to that position. By the 1970s, however, a policy that denied women entrance to a publicly funded institution appeared increasingly problematic. What to some qualified as hallowed tradition, to others amounted to flagrant discrimination. Congressional action in 1975 obliging the service academies to admit women—the vote was 303–96 in the House of Representatives with Senate passage by a voice vote—established a pattern of sorts: while welcoming larger numbers of women into their ranks, the army and other services nonetheless resolved to preserve certain all-male enclaves, to which feminists in and out of uniform promptly laid siege, forcing the services to retreat farther.[10] The enclaves of masculine exclusivity grew ever smaller.

In waging this fruitless campaign, the army was its own worst enemy. Recurring episodes involving sexual misconduct by male soldiers occupying positions of authority grabbed public attention, leaving the service constantly on the defensive. In 1996, at a major army training installation, eleven drill sergeants (and one officer) were charged with harassing female trainees. Among the accusations: trainers had granted favorable treatment in return for sex. Hard on the heels of this so-called Aberdeen Scandal came an even greater embarrassment: a female NCO with over twenty years' service charged the sergeant major of the army—the service's senior enlisted soldier—with a pattern of harassment. The ensuing court-martial of Command Sergeant Major Gene McKinney generated a cascade of adverse publicity.[11] So, too, did the case of a general officer accused of preying on the wives of his subordinates. In 1999, the army recalled retired Major General David Hale to active duty, investigated the charges, and, after a plea deal, reduced him in rank—with the press again paying careful attention.[12] Hale was not the sole general officer offender. Later that same year, the army charged Major General John Maher with propositioning a female enlisted soldier and sleeping with the wives of his immediate subordinates. He ended up losing both his stars and left active duty as a colonel.[13]

Worse was to come. In 2000, the army's highest-ranking woman—Lieutenant General Claudia Kennedy—charged a two-star colleague with making unwelcome advances in her own Pentagon office. The accused, Major General Larry Smith, eventually received a letter of reprimand, forfeited his announced promotion to three-star rank, and was obliged to retire.[14] Again, all of this occurred with a full blast of unwelcome media attention. Hitherto all but unknown, General Kennedy became a heroine and a well-regarded public figure.[15]

In part due to these successive waves of negative publicity, issues related to women in the military remained an especially active front in the ongoing culture wars. Book-length polemics questioned whether a feminized military would remain capable of winning the nation's wars.[16] James Webb, highly decorated Vietnam veteran, best-selling novelist, former Pentagon official, and future senator, emerged as the most vocal exponent of this critique. For Webb, himself a naval academy graduate, the admission of women to the service academies had marked the opening salvo in what had become a decades-long campaign by "sociologists, agenda feminists, and a small core of political-activist military officers" seeking "to destroy the military culture from the outside." Willing to grant women a role in military service, Webb was intent on excluding them from combat as such. Effectiveness in that environment, he insisted, depended in considerable part on small-unit cohesion, based on male-male bonding. Male-female relationships were inevitably about sex. Admit women into combat units and cohesion would fall victim to "the sexual jealousies, courtship rituals, and favoritism that are the hallmarks of romantic relationships." Webb viewed the assault on traditional military culture as a proxy war, an offshoot of the larger ongoing effort to subvert American culture.

> In its drive for ratification of the Equal Rights Amendment, the feminist movement saw the military as its optimal "peripheral" battle. To win on the issue of women in combat, the most quintessentially male obligation in any society, would moot all other debates regarding female roles. For many males who did not serve [in Vietnam], particularly the high achievers who wished no blemish on their reputations, the "demasculinization" of the military was a natural deterrent to any attack on their manhood as their youthful actions came to be viewed in retrospect.[17]

Yet well before Webb advanced his argument, the very concept of a "quintessentially male obligation" had already become extinct. The problem with Webb's formulation lay not with the adverb or adjective but with the noun. Two decades earlier, a young female recruit had succinctly captured the essence of the matter: "If there's another war, we'll be there," she told a reporter, "because with this voluntary system the men who don't want to be here aren't here."[18] Male and female alike, Americans had abandoned collective obligation in favor of personal choice. Thanks to Richard Nixon, this applied to soldiering no less than to other pursuits.

In effect, Webb and his fellow traditionalists found themselves in the position of segregationists in the 1960s, still citing states' rights as a basis for maintaining racial separation. Except among diehards, the argument no longer retained any standing.

Like the other services, a reluctant army found itself with little choice but to cede to the politics of gender. Incrementally, over the course of several decades, restrictions on the duty positions open to women fell away. By 9/11, few such limits remained apart from a prohibition on specialties associated with close combat, primarily crewing armored vehicles and assignment as infantry.

Not surprisingly, during the Iraq War of 2003–11, women soldiers played a prominent role, both on and off the battlefield. They engaged the enemy. They were shot down. They were taken prisoner.[19] They suffered grievous wounds. They won awards for gallantry.[20] They succumbed to barbarity, Private Lynndie England becoming the face of the Abu Ghraib scandal. They were found wanting, Brigadier General Janis Karpinski, Abu Ghraib commander, enjoying the unhappy distinction of being the only U.S. general officer to be demoted for poor performance in Iraq. Yet overall they performed admirably, even if sometimes their very best efforts were not good enough. When my son was killed in Iraq, one of the medics attending him was a woman.

Increasing the number of women in the war zone and assigning them to duties on or near the front lines has this added consequence: when the United States goes to war, the list of those making the ultimate sacrifice now inevitably includes women. During the Iraq War, for example, 110 female uniformed personnel died for their country (that total including both those killed in action and fatalities from nonhostile causes).[21] For friends and family of the deceased, that statistic signifies 110 individual stories of crushing, irreparable loss. Yet in a perverse sense, it also represents progress—one measure of the fruit borne by the progressive elimination of gender discrimination within the armed forces.[22]

Still, even if more female soldiers were dying, they were not yet doing so at a rate remotely equivalent to that of their male counterparts. Roughly 15 percent of the total force, women made up a mere 2.5 percent of the fatalities sustained in Iraq.[23] (In Afghanistan, as of May 2012, 1.5 percent of total U.S. military losses were female.)[24] From the perspective of ensuring full equality, these figures showed that there remained work to do, with the signs of the times all suggesting that a gender-neutral fighting force was in the offing. "We are the most civilized nation in the world that still formally excludes women from combat," the Boston Globe columnist Juliette Kayyem complained.[25] That the United States would soon catch up with the rest of the civilized world in this regard seemed a foregone conclusion. To hasten that day, female officers in 2012 sued the army, charging that barring them from combat violated their constitutional rights, above all the right to exercise individual choice.[26] "We all should be able to choose how we pursue our careers and what conditions we want to subject ourselves to," one of the plaintiffs explained. "We can't have a policy that says I'm not allowed to compete."[27]

As if in direct response, that very same year army chief of staff General Raymond Odierno signaled his interest in enrolling women in the army's elite Ranger School, a preliminary step toward gender integrating infantry units. Women Rangers, he explained, would be more "competitive with their male counterparts as they move through the ranks."[28] Given the convergence of gender politics, emphasizing empowerment and self-actualization, with the imperative of sustaining the all-volunteer force, where women have become essential, ensuring "competitiveness"—that is, prospects for individual advancement—had become an overriding priority.[29] General Martin Dempsey, chairman of the Joint Chiefs of

Staff, concurred. Emphasizing the imperative of every member of the military, regardless of gender, being "given the opportunity to succeed," Dempsey urged Secretary of Defense Leon Panetta in January 2013 to abolish all remaining restrictions on where women would serve. Panetta issued the necessary directive forthwith.[30]

Once upon a time, feminists had believed that breaking the bonds of patriarchy might contribute to war's elimination, the liberation of women making the world not only a different place but also a better place, to the benefit of all humankind. The closer women come to the goal of full equality, the less likely any such outcome appears. In the case of the United States, with the supply of male volunteers insufficient to sustain the nation's armed forces, militarists who care about little apart from sustaining a capacity for global military action and feminists obsessed with eliminating all vestiges of discrimination have forged an improbable alliance. As a consequence, the ongoing campaign for gender equality sustains rather than undercuts America's propensity for war. Hitherto a blight laid at the feet of men, war is becoming an activity that allows women a full share in the bloodletting, this constituting, in the words of one *Washington Post* columnist, "the painful and real price of true equality."[31]

DON'T (EVEN) ASK

If army leaders responded with something less than enthusiasm to demands for full gender equality, there was no doubting the position they staked out in response to the possibility of allowing homosexuals and lesbians to serve. It was an emphatic no: negative, no way, no how, never.

In fact, this particular issue ranked as a nonissue until the presidential election of 1992. From a martial perspective, that contest featured the most radical mismatch since 1900, when William McKinley, Civil War hero and architect of a seemingly "splendid little war" against Spain, had faced off against William Jennings Bryan, possessing negligible soldierly credentials. Ninety-some years later, George H. W. Bush, World War II hero and architect of a seemingly "splendid little war" with Saddam Hussein's Iraq, faced off against William Jefferson Clinton, the governor of Arkansas. Although inclined toward pacifism, Bryan in 1898 had impulsively enlisted in the Nebraska National Guard, hoping to participate in the liberation of Cuba. He got no closer to the war zone than Florida. No such warrior impulsiveness ever got the better of Bill Clinton, who exerted himself strenuously, successfully, and without evident remorse to avoid military service during the Vietnam War.

Yet Clinton was an exceedingly gifted politician who, with the fortuitous assistance of a mild economic recession, turned an election that incumbent Bush should have won in a walk into an upset victory. As part of his political strategy, Clinton emphasized his resolute commitment to equal opportunity for all Americans, the definition of *all* now encompassing not only race, creed, ethnicity, and gender but also sexual orientation.

Gay rights was becoming a hot-button issue, the heat arising in considerable part from the fierce hostility of American conservatives toward anything that smacked of normalizing homosexuality. By no means incidentally, the post–Cold War officer corps was as shot through with cultural conservatism as any major group to the left of Bible Belt evangelicals. So when Clinton at a Seattle campaign stop in the summer of 1992 promised to restore to duty a former reservist forced to leave military service after she had admitted to being a lesbian—and by extension to lift the prohibition on gays serving openly in the military—he unwittingly put himself on a collision course with the armed forces of the United States.[32]

Once elected, Clinton immediately signaled his intention to keep this particular campaign promise.[33] The officer corps wasted no time in indicating its displeasure with that prospect. General Colin Powell, the highly regarded chairman of the Joint Chiefs of Staff, bluntly stated that removing the ban on gays serving openly in the military "would be prejudicial to good order and discipline."[34]

By Clinton's inauguration, gays-in-the-military had displaced ongoing crises in Bosnia and Somalia as issue number one in the eyes of senior U.S. military leaders. The question dominated the first meeting between newly appointed Secretary of Defense Les Aspin and the Joint Chiefs, who immediately (if anonymously) shared with reporters their conviction "that repealing the ban would wreck morale, undermine recruiting, force devoutly religious service members to resign and increase the risk of AIDS for heterosexual troops."[35] As the controversy mushroomed, a dispute over policy took on wider significance, raising questions relating to civilian control of the military and posing a test of character for the newly elected president. Here, the New York Times editorialized, was "a chance for Mr. Clinton to show that the anti-war student from Arkansas has the spine to be Commander in Chief."[36]

As it turned out, Clinton passed on the opportunity, opting instead to back away from a fight that he seemed destined to lose. The result was "don't ask, don't tell," a compromise brokered by congressional Democrats not sharing the president's commitment to gay rights. The new policy—making explicit a practice that had hitherto been implicit—permitted gays to serve in the armed forces as long as they concealed their sexual orientation. In a remarkable display of political muscle-flexing, the brass had bested their commander in chief.

Matters did not end there, however. For the gay rights movement, "don't ask, don't tell"—or DADT, as it came to be known—

turned out to be the defeat that planted the seeds of ultimate victory. Setback became springboard. DADT provided a rallying cry that mobilized supporters, pried open wallets, and ultimately recast the terms of debate, both morally and politically. Alone among the population of able-bodied Americans, out-of-the-closet gays were prohibited from volunteering for military service. In a culture that increasingly celebrated individual autonomy as the supreme value, this proved to be an untenable proposition.

So the issue refused to go away. On otherwise somnolent college campuses DADT became a bona fide cause, the basis for considerable posturing by senior administrators. Deans and presidents demonstrated their opposition to DADT by steadfastly refusing to allow ROTC on campus or by barring the Pentagon from official participation in on-campus job fairs. "I abhor the military's discriminatory recruitment policy," future Supreme Court justice Elena Kagan assured Harvard Law School students and faculty upon becoming dean in 2003. "This is a profound wrong—a moral injustice of the first order," one that "tears at the fabric of our own community, because some of our members cannot, while others can, devote their professional careers to their country."[37] Yet at Harvard and elsewhere, efforts to redress this profound moral wrong were pursued in ways that carefully protected the university's access to federal research funds. Although opposing DADT on principle, elite institutions like Harvard were not going to allow principle to impede their harvesting of taxpayer dollars.

Arguably more influential were the efforts of organizations such as the Servicemembers Legal Defense Network (SLDN), founded in 1993, and the Center for the Study of Sexual Minorities in the Military, founded in 1998 and subsequently renamed the Palm Center. SLDN provided free legal assistance to military members subjected to harassment or discrimination on the basis of sexual orientation, its client list eventually numbering in the thousands. It also lobbied Congress to repeal "don't ask, don't tell." For its part, the Palm Center critically scrutinized General Powell's hypothesis (shared by other senior officers) that allowing uncloseted gays to serve would undermine military effectiveness. Not too surprisingly, its researchers reached different conclusions.[38]

Meanwhile, in the larger culture, the normalization of homosexuality continued apace. In remarkably short order, homophobia joined anti-Semitism, racism, and sexism on the short list of unforgivable sins. However modestly, the continuing controversy engendered by DADT helped promote this change. To a perhaps greater degree, growing popular discomfort with any form of discrimination targeting gays made their exclusion from military service seem an outrageous affront. In 1992–93, generals opposed to allowing gays to serve openly could portray themselves as shielding the United States military from assault by the forces of political correctness. Hardly more than a decade later, DADT's defenders came across as wildly out of touch, if not positively un-American—latter-day George Wallaces reenacting the Alabama governor's infamous 1963 stand in the schoolhouse door.

The requirements of waging the never-ending Global War on Terrorism also played a role in undermining DADT. With Arab linguists in desperately short supply, how could it make sense to discharge soldiers studying Arabic simply because of their sexual orientation?[39] Booting gays out of the army was not enhancing national security. If anything, the reverse appeared true. An army dependent on volunteers could no more do without lesbians and homosexuals than it could do without blacks and women. To pretend otherwise was to play into the hands of America's enemies. Such was the argument anyway. Almost overnight, the mantle of patriotism passed from those who supported DADT to those who opposed it.

By 2010, military leaders were ready to throw in their heteronormative towel. Allowing that "attitudes and circumstances have changed," General Powell, now retired, reversed his position and declared his support for repealing "don't ask, don't tell."[40] Admiral Mike Mullen, Joint Chiefs chairman at the time, concurred, as did Secretary of Defense Robert Gates. When a TV reporter asked where he stood on the matter, General David Petraeus, then as well regarded as Powell had once been, professed not to understand what all the fuss was about.[41]

With that, DADT's days were numbered. Much as Nixon had done once he had decided to jettison the draft, the Pentagon made a show of deliberation, in this instance by "consulting" the troops.[42] (On genuinely important matters like whether to go to war, no one has ever much cared about opinion in the ranks.) When the troops ventured no objection, the stage was set to end DADT, which following congressional action and with presidential approval finally became defunct on September 20, 2011. In the intervening eighteen years, the Pentagon had discharged approximately 14,500 servicemen and servicewomen under its provisions.[43]

For gay rights proponents, DADT's demise signified a notable victory. For the military itself, it turned out to be a nonevent.[44] Months later, Mullen's successor as JCS chairman, army General Martin Dempsey, could discern no "negative effect on good order or discipline." On the sexual orientation front, all appeared quiet. Asked why the prospect of gays serving openly had once elicited such fierce opposition from senior officers, Dempsey cited bias reinforced by ignorance. "What were we afraid of is [what] we didn't know."[45]

IN STEP

However belatedly, the army, along with the rest of the armed services, had once again bowed to the prevailing normative winds,

much as it had already done on race and gender. Still, the Pentagon's capitulation on DADT had its own special significance. In
this instance, the viability of the all-volunteer force was never
really at stake. In practice, the army and the other services do not
need gays any more than they need Ivy Leaguers—the numbers
involved are not large enough to make a decisive difference. Nor
was striking sexual orientation from the criteria determining eli-
gibility for military service going to induce droves of gays to enlist,
thereby making life easy for recruiting sergeants. Just as female
soldiers didn't turn the army pink, so allowing gays to serve openly
is unlikely to produce a mauve-tinted military. Fort Bragg or Fort
Benning won't be replacing San Francisco's Castro district or Key
West as favored gay watering holes anytime soon.

Yet the no-big-deal attitude that the Pentagon projected as it
dismantled DADT concealed a very big deal indeed. Here, as far as
relations between the army and society were concerned, the Long
Sixties reached their denouement. The civil-military antagonisms
to which that turbulent era gave rise, compounded by Vietnam
and expressed most fiercely in opposition to the draft, were now
finally laid to rest. Over the course of four decades, largely for reasons of self-preservation, the army had adapted itself to social and
cultural changes that the 1960s had wrought. An institution that
in 1971 had seemed badly out of step with society was by 2011 in
lockstep on the defining social issues of the day. On matters related
to race, gender, and sexual orientation, the army had caught up
with the rest of the country and appeared none the worse for wear.

Now, in direct response to DADT's repeal, institutions where
the trinity of race, gender, and sexuality had become most deeply
enshrined offered the military an olive branch of sorts. The result,
expressed by the highly publicized decision of (some) elite universities to end ROTC's Vietnam-induced exile from campus, may
not have qualified as genuine reconciliation. But as an armistice

that served the interests of all parties, it seemed likely to hold indefinitely.

Providing the foundation for that armistice was a new civil-military bargain. Harvard president Drew Faust accurately captured its essence. "The repeal of DADT," she announced approvingly, "affirms American ideals of equal opportunity and underscores the importance of the right to military service as a fundamental dimension of citizenship."[46] At Harvard, as at other elite colleges and universities, few students were clamoring to exercise any such right. Still, to validate and affirm its existence, Faust promised that, after a decades-long absence, ROTC would be returning to Harvard. With the Pentagon having tacitly acknowledged a universal right to serve, Harvard would not abridge that right.

As Faust's formulation suggests, individual choice had now fully eclipsed state power as the principal determinant of who will defend the country. The end of conscription had shorn the state of its authority to *compel* service. The evolving identity of the all-volunteer force, culminating in the abandonment of DADT, progressively curtailed the state's authority to *deny* individuals the option of serving, except on narrowly drawn grounds of mental or physical ability.[47] The conversion of military service from collective obligation to personal preference was now complete and irrevocable. With that, an army that in the 1960s had been politically radioactive became politically inert—of no more importance in national domestic politics than the Bureau of Indian Affairs or the Forest Service.

6

SEARCHING FOR DRAGONS TO SLAY

By accommodating demands for social and cultural change, the army succeeded in restoring its legitimacy in the eyes of American society. That achievement, however, came at a cost, even if few observers contemplated the implications. By no stretch of the imagination did the all-volunteer army qualify as—or seek to be—an army of the people. Now culturally in step, it was content to march alongside, but at arm's length from, the rest of American society. At the time, this arrangement suited most Americans just fine.

For military leaders, such a distance had its benefits. In matters relating to war's actual conduct, the officer corps continued to exercise at least nominal authority. Drew Faust might instruct the military on how to treat gays and lesbians, but when it came to preparing and organizing to fight she deferred to those with stars on their shoulders. Deciding how to train American infantrymen remained the business of army officers at Fort Benning, not academics in Harvard Yard.

Social and cultural accommodation also helped restore a sense of discipline within the ranks. With time, the internal divisions that had wracked the army as Vietnam wound down—blacks versus whites, dopers versus drinkers, lifers versus short-timers—healed. The collective dissent and overt challenges to authority that prompted flummoxed commanders to host "rap sessions" or add "soul food" to mess hall menus dissipated. By the end of the twentieth century, the Vietnam-era afflictions besieging the army had largely washed out of the system. The chain of command was once again just that.

These achievements—legitimacy restored and discipline reasserted—ensured the viability of the all-volunteer force. Indeed, they made any alternative to such a military essentially unimaginable. Transitioning from the draft to this new arrangement had not occurred without missteps. Yet as with the memory of a bad hangover following a night of excess, the urge to move on, suppressing any recollection of past embarrassments, was overwhelming.

The army proved less adept at accommodating—or even understanding—a second revolution, a geopolitical one touched off by the passing of the Cold War. For decades, the standoff between opposing superpowers had provided the lens through which Americans, elites and ordinary people alike, interpreted international politics. Soviet power and the ambitions ascribed to Soviet leaders from Joseph Stalin to Leonid Brezhnev had served as an all-purpose rationale for the vast national security apparatus created in the wake of World War II. Prior to 1945, the United States had shied away from maintaining a large, permanent military establishment. Except in times of actual hostilities, popular reluctance to support an army worthy of the name had been particularly acute. After 1945, however, this changed. Americans convinced themselves that the challenge posed by the Soviet Union and the forces of global communism left them with no choice but to field an immense warfighting establishment, including large ground forces geared for combat. For nearly a half century, standing ready to fight the Soviet hordes had provided the United States Army with its overarching raison d'être.

After years lost wandering in the jungles and rice paddies of Vietnam, the army's preoccupation with the Red Army returned with a vengeance. By the 1980s, the last vestiges of "Elvis's army"—the draftee force that had deployed to Southeast Asia—had disappeared.[1] In its place there emerged "Abe's army," its cigar-chomping patron saint General Creighton Abrams. Successor to William Westmoreland as U.S. commander in Vietnam and then as army chief of staff, Abrams died prematurely in 1974, with the army he loved still very much trying to regain its footing. Yet a generation of true-believing disciples carried on his work, fired by a common determination to exorcise the demons of Vietnam.

The overall aim, unspoken but widely understood, was for the officer corps to reclaim control of the army's destiny. With that in mind, Abe's disciples intended to fight only those wars mattering enough to attract the nation's full backing. This consideration determined the army's organization. Furthermore, they intended to fight only wars that conformed to their conception of what war itself should be, with victory once more the aim. This consideration shaped operational doctrine.

No more getting hung out to dry. No more serving as the plaything of meddling civilian officials. No more long, drawn-out inconclusive conflicts. This describes Abe's vision, which became the army's as a whole. The place that held the prospect of fulfilling that vision was not some Third World country but Europe, where Abe himself had first won plaudits as a hard-charging armored force commander during World War II and where Russians, rather than their Asian "proxies," would be the foe.

Creating Abe's army entailed a collaborative effort involving many hands. Among the collaborators, none possessed greater value than the Soviet Union itself. Abe's army needed the Red Army, the more fearsome the better. For an officer corps committed to avoiding any recurrence of Vietnam, the Soviets and their Warsaw Pact allies provided an invaluable "other." Preparing to fight Russians was a gift that promised never to stop giving, the ready-made answer to every question essential to institutional recovery and continued health. An expansionist Soviet empire, its mighty legions armed to the teeth with a massive arsenal of modern weapons, was just what the doctor ordered.[2]

Unfortunately, the Soviets proved unwilling to keep up their end of the arrangement. Reliably obdurate for decades, over the course of the 1980s they became disconcertingly amenable. A decade of progressive threat deflation ensued, with the Kremlin embracing liberalizing reforms, signing treaties to reduce nuclear weapons stocks, and announcing huge unilateral cuts—five hundred thousand troops—to its Eastern Europe garrisons. In 1989, the Soviets stood passively by as the Berlin Wall fell, with German unification following shortly thereafter. In 1991, the Warsaw Pact, paramount symbol of Soviet hegemony in Eastern Europe, dissolved. That same year, so did the Soviet Union.

For Abe's army, the good news was the bad news: mission accomplished, without any actual fighting, no less. Now what?

The collapse of the Soviet empire presented Americans with a rare opportunity to pose first-order questions about their nation's proper role in the world and by extension about the size, configuration, and disposition of its armed forces. As some observers saw it, with the Cold War over, the American people could rightly expect to claim a reward—a "peace dividend"—in the form of a more modest military posture and reduced military spending. After all, Europe, the central focus of Abe's army, was now whole and free. As for the dwindling roster of communist regimes, they were either like Cuba too sclerotic to worry about or like China too economically dynamic to quarrel with.

Along with the rest of the national security apparatus, the army had a powerful interest in curbing Washington's inclination to distribute any such dividend. For the Pentagon, peace posed a concrete and imminent threat. Generals who had slept undisturbed back when Warsaw Pact commanders had ostensibly been planning to launch World War III now fretted nervously over the prospect of their budget taking a hit. The most obvious way to deflect that prospect was to conjure up new dangers to which only Abe's army could offer the necessary response. In Saddam Hussein, Abe's disciples found a made-to-order helpmate.

SADDAM AND SULLY TO THE RESCUE

Responsibility for formulating a definition of purpose to replace the Cold War while discovering a new adversary to replace the Red Army fell primarily on the shoulders of General Gordon R. Sullivan, army chief of staff from 1991 to 1995. During his tenure as the service's most senior officer, Sullivan wrote, or allowed to appear under his name, a series of essays in official journals, most prominently *Military Review*, published at Fort Leavenworth, Kansas. These articles, along with the writings of Sullivan's three-star and four-star contemporaries, record the army's response to the passing of the Cold War.

In a memoir, Sullivan recalled watching the fall of the Berlin Wall, as broadcast by CNN. "It was momentous. It was as if we were IBM contemplating the first Apple computer, or General Motors the first Volkswagen or Toyota."[3] The comparisons were revealing. IBM had been producing computers for decades before Steve Jobs unveiled his first creation. It would continue to do so for decades to come. Much the same could be said about General Motors as it confronted the challenge posed by cheap, high-quality imports. GM was not going to quit making cars, but preserving its standing in that business meant adapting to new conditions.

So, too, with the army after the Cold War. Its leaders spoke in terms of revolutionary upheaval while actually pursuing a course of incremental adaptation. The aim of adaptation was fundamentally conservative: to preserve the army's status within the national security establishment and its standing in the eyes of society, or as Sullivan put it, "to take the best army in the world and make it the best army in a different world."[4]

Army leaders understood that, with the end of the Cold War, their service was going to be "much smaller."[5] Yet they were intent on investing this smaller force—which was still going to be far larger than any pre–Cold War "peacetime" army—with the capacity to take on "new, expanded and diverse missions."[6] In essence, the post–Cold War army was going to do more with less and was going to do it better than any armed force in history. To demonstrate their service's continued relevance, army leaders were keen to put soldiers to work, taking on new assignments in unfamiliar places. Sullivan might note "the paradox of declining military resources and increasing military missions," but neither he nor his general officer colleagues found the implications of that paradox especially troubling.[7]

In describing and promoting this new agenda, senior officers relied less on empirical evidence and analytical rigor than on attitude. They projected confidence, occasionally laced with bluster. "The 'World's Best Army' is a bumper sticker," wrote one four-star general, "but it is a bumper sticker we deserve and have earned."[8]

Divining the army's future yielded an abundance of lists: five "tenets" (agility, initiative, depth, synchronization, and versatility) intended to guide doctrine;[9] five "warning lights" indicative of fundamental change, which pointed toward five "new concepts" for combat;[10] not to mention, five "modernization thrusts,"[11] supplemented by five "modernization objectives;"[12] and when it came to leadership, five "C's" (commitment, courage, candor, competence, and compassion).[13] Lest all this suggest a fixation on the number five, the authoritative list of "core combat capabilities" consisted of just four items,[14] whereas the "beacon" guiding the army toward the future derived its power to illuminate from six "enduring imperatives."[15]

Embedded in this mania for enumeration was an argument of sorts. Its aim was to establish the service's continuing and indeed expanded relevance to U.S. national security policy. If only for reasons of symmetry, we will distill that argument into five essential points.

First, as far as Sullivan and other army leaders were concerned, the demise of the Soviet empire was at best a mixed blessing and perhaps no blessing at all. Rather than paving the way for peace on Earth, the passing of the Cold War had triggered instability, creating a host of new threats. Within two years of the Soviet Union's demise, Sullivan had discerned that the world was "growing more dangerous." By way of elaboration, he cited a litany of problems: "ethnic and religious hostility, weapons proliferation, power struggles created by the disappearance of the Soviet Union, elimination of the fear of regional conflicts escalating to superpower confrontation, radicalisms of a number of varieties, rising expectations of democracy and free markets coupled with the inability of governments to meet those expectations."[16]

He did not invent this litany. In 1990s Washington, it was standard fare. So, too, was the conviction that the resulting tumult demanded a concerted response from the sole surviving superpower. Here was a new world disorder to which the U.S. military was going to have to attend.

General Carl Vuono, Sullivan's predecessor as chief of staff, had already made a similar point. The post–Cold War era, he believed, promised to be one of great "uncertainty and peril." In 1990, the Iraqi invasion of Kuwait had provided "a vivid preview of the nature of the international system in the decade of the 1990s and beyond."[17] For Vuono's fellow generals, the preview was not only vivid but exceedingly welcome.

For Abe's army, Saddam Hussein's Iraq offered an ideal adversary, far more attractive, in crucial respects, than the old Soviet Union. In reconstituting itself after Vietnam, the army had labored mightily to refute the reigning popular impression that war inevitably resulted in little more than pointless destruction. Put another way, making a plausible case that U.S. forces along with their NATO allies could save Europe without having to destroy it (along with the rest of the planet) had become an imperative. Any conflict involving the large-scale use of nuclear weapons—which NATO and the Warsaw Pact both possessed in abundance—would necessarily fail to meet that standard.

To escape this dilemma, planners assumed it away: World War III, they had posited, would begin with a conventional invasion of Western Europe, both sides choosing to refrain from using their nuclear arsenals. That assumption was always improbable. In retrospect, we know it was false. The Warsaw Pact had every intention of employing nuclear weapons at the outset of any showdown with NATO.[18] Yet at the time, assuming otherwise was too useful to gainsay.

With Iraq, the poster nation for a new threat category that Washington had dubbed "rogue states," no such legerdemain was necessary. Rogue states, including Iran and North Korea along with Iraq, might covet nuclear weapons, but they did not (yet) possess them. Indeed, their nuclear aspirations, by definition illegitimate and posing a danger to world peace, confirmed their status as suitable foes. As long as aspirations did not become capabilities, the army could expect to fight on terms of its liking.

Despite the collapse of communism, in short, peace remained an illusion. Abe's army was going to have plenty of work to do, precisely as he and his collaborators had intended. With exquisite timing, Saddam Hussein made that point eminently clear.

Second, as Washington came to appreciate the significance of these new threats, army leaders foresaw the prospect of greater American activism. With the end of the Cold War, containment had become obsolete. It no longer sufficed. The Iraqi invasion of Kuwait in 1990, Vuono predicted, would "be remembered for generations to come as a turning point . . . the day America announced the end of containment and embarked upon the strategy of power projection."[19] By projecting military power, Washington would nip problems in the bud or at least prevent them from getting out of hand. "The United States no longer has a negative aim," wrote Sullivan. "It has a positive aim—to promote democracy, regional stability, and economic prosperity." As far as military policy was concerned, "prevention" was supplanting "deterrence."[20]

Third, charged with what Vuono called a "global strategic mandate," the army was intent on claiming a large part of the Pentagon's power-projection portfolio.[21] Rather than ceding ground to the navy or air force, wrote one general, "we need to arrive with the élan of a confident proven winner moving to an attack position, about to master new horizons." After all, the static posture to which the army had become accustomed during the latter part of the Cold War—garrisoning Western Europe and South Korea— had been "an aberration in our national military history." Emerging threats dictated that the army should henceforth maintain "a highly-ready, highly-visible rapid intervention capability."[22]

Sullivan believed it incumbent upon the army to serve as the nation's "principal instrument for the projection of carefully modulated military force." After all, the United States could not rely on sea power or airpower to bring its wars to a successful conclusion. History had repeatedly shown that "it is the commitment of ground force in the decisive terrain that finally resolves the contest of will that we call war."[23] Or as another four-star put it, "We are now pursuing a power-projection strategy . . . guided by the view that land combat remains decisive in war."[24]

Fourth, armed conflict—whether the large-scale clash of ground forces or any of the lesser contingencies that the Pentagon styled Operations Other Than War (OOTW)—could have but a single acceptable outcome: unambiguous success. In 1991, Sullivan wrote, "we must be a strategic force capable of decisive victory."[25] In 1992, he became more insistent: "[We] will be a strategic force capable of decisive victory."[26] The basic operational manual, revised the following year, removed any lingering ambiguity on the question. "Victory," it stated categorically, "is the objective no matter what the mission. Nothing short of victory is acceptable."[27]

In fact, merely winning was not enough. The requirement was to prevail with speed and economy, achieving "national objectives quickly and with minimal expenditure of national wealth and resources." America, Sullivan wrote, "does not expect protracted, attrition warfare."[28] This was setting the bar high indeed. Yet to demonstrate the feasibility of this demanding standard, Sullivan pointed to Operation Desert Storm, when America's army had handily defeated "the fourth largest army in the world in 100 hours."[29]

Finally, what endowed this approach with a semblance of plausibility was a belief in the transformative implications of information technology. The onset of the 1990s marked the flowering of the Information Age. Americans were falling in love with the Network. So, too, was the Pentagon. The army, Sullivan asserted, was "on the leading edge of the revolution in military affairs."[30] Information—acquiring it, analyzing it, sharing it—held "the key to a vast improvement in effectiveness." Information was making it possible to apply force more rapidly and with greater precision. Job one in any conflict was to "win the information war," thereby enabling army forces "to apply power to the main effort quickly, to attack the enemy simultaneously throughout the battle area, and . . . to do it over and over again, allowing him no time to react, recover, or regroup."[31] According to Sullivan, "overmatching technology" would provide the means "to apply overwhelming and decisive combat power while minimizing risks to our soldiers."[32] Here, Sullivan's army parted company with Abe's, indulging fantasies about the transformative potential of technology that General Abrams would have derided as preposterous.

For Sullivan and other army leaders, one specific episode during Operation Desert Storm sufficed as proof of concept. Late in the afternoon of February 26, 1991, an armored cavalry troop commanded by Captain H. R. McMaster encountered an Iraqi mechanized brigade. In the ensuing fight—subsequently enshrined as the Battle of 73 Easting[33]—McMaster's much smaller company-sized unit destroyed something like thirty Soviet-built T72 tanks along with several dozen trucks and personnel carriers, all in about an hour. Enemy soldiers who weren't killed just gave up, handing themselves over to captivity. When the fight concluded, it left few loose ends. All but unscratched, the U.S. force sustained *no* casualties.[34] Here, army leaders quickly concluded, was an event comparable in its historical significance to the action at Gettysburg's Little Round Top or the storming of Omaha Beach—a successful engagement validating the recent past while pointing to an even more promising future.[35]

In fact, the Battle of Omdurman might have provided a more apt comparison. In that 1898 clash between British regulars and a badly overmatched Sudanese army, a technological disparity had indeed proven decisive. The Brits had machine guns and artillery, whereas the Sudanese had none. Yet if British commanders fancied that by slaughtering ten thousand Mahdists they had thereby mastered the art of war, the Boers (not to mention the Germans) would soon demonstrate otherwise. Still, in the wake of Desert Storm, this was ancient history for an American army eager to see in 73 Easting profound lessons of universal applicability. Advanced technology in the hands of well-trained troops offered, it seemed, a recipe for designing forces able to run rings around any opponent.

The challenge was to scale up, creating an entire army capable of doing in any environment and against any opponent what Captain McMaster's doughty band had accomplished against a not-especially-competent Iraqi adversary. With that goal in mind, army leaders conceived something called Force XXI, a template for converting Sullivan's vision into reality. This was, in effect, an elaborate experiment intended to corroborate conclusions Sullivan had already reached. The mandate from on high was not "find out what works" but "confirm that this works."

Needless to say, the characteristics that the army sought to embed in Force XXI were five in number: "doctrinal flexibility; strategic mobility; tailorability and modularity; joint, multinational, and interagency connectivity; and versatility in war and OOTW."[36] These elephantine phrases concealed the full extent of the program's ambitions, which were little short of utopian. By "pushing the envelope and transforming today's very good Army into an even better information age, knowledge- and capabilities-based Army," one three-star enthusiast wrote, the United States would enjoy "land force dominance across the continuum of 21st century military operations." This, he concluded, "is what Force XXI is all about."[37]

LESSONS OVERLOOKED AND IGNORED

Commingling facts, assertions, and aspirations seldom produces clarity. Yet the promoters of Sullivan's doing-more-with-less-and-doing-it-better-than-ever approach mixed together the known, the assumed, and the hoped for with abandon.

As any car salesman will tell you, careful selection and sculpting determine which facts count—and which don't. So sustaining the claim, for instance, that in 1991 U.S. ground forces had defeated "the fourth largest army in the world in 100 hours" meant overlooking the several weeks of uncontested aerial bombardment to which Iraqi forces were subjected before the coalition ground attack began. Similarly, to keep the WORLD'S BEST ARMY bumper sticker unbesmirched, it helped to ignore the ignominious spanking of a ranger task force administered by a Somali warlord in 1993. Tagging civilian policy makers with the blame for the disastrous "Blackhawk Down" firefight in Mogadishu rendered that episode irrelevant except as a testament to the gallantry of American soldiers.[38]

Treating assertions as if they were facts enhances their persuasiveness. In reality, Iraq's 1990 invasion of Kuwait turned out to be less a harbinger than an anomalous throwback—the sort of boneheaded move only someone as imprudent as Saddam Hussein would make. Yet styling the Iraq War as a "preview" of things to come endowed what was in most ways a trivial event with exalted significance. It became a "turning point," with figures in authority wasting no time in explaining what that turn signified. So, too, with the army's putative "global strategic mandate," to which the Persian Gulf War gave birth. The very construction of the phrase— global = expansive, strategic = weighty, mandate = ordered from on high—aimed to silence doubts and deflect skeptical questions. What demanded priority attention was the mandate's fulfillment.

As for aspirations, bigger is always better. The goal that Sullivan's army set for itself was positively breathtaking: No more long wars. No more costly wars. No more futile or unsuccessful wars. Just neat, tidy ones, ending in absolute and unquestioned triumph.

Granted, no army in modern history had been able to meet this standard, but as Sullivan and his fellow generals saw it, history no longer bound the troops that they led. The advent of Force XXI, as they imagined it, was going to make the otherwise fanciful eminently doable. Seldom if ever has a group of seasoned, otherwise sober military professionals succumbed more thoroughly or willingly to the seductive sound of their own voices.

In fact, Sullivan's case was weakest where he and his fellow generals believed it to be strongest—in their depiction of Operation Desert Storm as both validation and precursor. Although the Persian Gulf War of 1990–91 had yielded a victory of sorts—the liberation of Kuwait being the principal fruit—the outcome qualified as *decisive* only by using the very loosest definition of that adjective.

The problem with depicting Operation Desert Storm as a "100-hour war" was not only that it ignored the bombing campaign that preceded the action on the ground. Of equal or greater importance was the fact that the war didn't really end when President George H. W. Bush ordered coalition forces to cease operations against Iraq's battered army. Operation Desert Storm settled very little, while leaving much unsettled. Given the strategic and political complications that ensued, the storied campaign of 1991 turned out to be merely the opening phase of a much longer and far more costly struggle.[39]

All of this appears blindingly obvious in retrospect. Whether historians ultimately classify U.S. military involvement in Iraq as a stand-alone event (a war for the Persian Gulf) or whether they situate it in a larger context (one part of the so-called Global War on Terrorism), the accompanying dates won't be those of Operation Desert Storm (January 17, 1991–February 28, 1991). Instead, that campaign signaled the firing of the first shots in a war destined to continue for two decades.[40]

However the debate about America's purposes in Iraq resolves itself—whether the aim was to "get the oil," deflect challenges to U.S. regional hegemony, liberate an oppressed people, or ensure the security of Israel—historians will be hard-pressed to conclude that U.S. military efforts in Mesopotamia *ever* resulted in anything akin to decisive victory. In 2011—some twenty years after Operation Desert Storm—President Obama spoke of U.S. forces leaving Iraq "with their heads held high, proud of their success, and knowing that the American people stand united in our support for our troops."[41] But *success* in this instance had become hardly more than a euphemism for the avoidance of utter defeat. Apart from a handful of deluded neoconservatives, no one believes that the United States accomplished its objectives in Iraq, unless the main objective was to commit mayhem, apply a tourniquet to staunch the bleeding, and then declare the patient stable while hastily leaving the scene of the crime.[42]

Yet even in the immediate wake of Desert Storm, which Sullivan and his colleagues were zealously enshrining as an all but flawless campaign, evidence suggesting otherwise was mounting.[43] Not that contrary evidence was going to dissuade senior army leaders from pursuing their vision of a smaller-but-better power-projection army with a global mandate. Like the naval officers for whom dreadnoughts had once represented the ultimate expression of seapower and the airpower advocates who proclaimed that the strategic bomber would always get through, they shut their eyes to whatever evidence they found inconvenient.

Yet facts evident at the time ought to have warned Pentagon leaders against nursing their utopian expectations. Those facts included not only the Somalia debacle (the true preview of things to come) but also the survival of Saddam Hussein's regime in Baghdad; the failed uprisings by Iraqi Shiites and Kurds after Desert Storm that saddled Washington with unforeseen enforcement and protection responsibilities; the emergence willy-nilly of a "dual containment" policy directed against both Iraq and Iran; and the establishment of a large-scale military presence in the Islamic world, inducing lethal blowback in the form of terrorist attacks directed against U.S. forces and American interests.[44]

The actual legacy of Desert Storm was to plunge the United States more deeply into a sea of difficulties for which military power provided no antidote. Yet in post–Cold War Washington, where *global leadership* and *global power projection* had become all but interchangeable terms, senior military officers like Sullivan were less interested in assessing what those difficulties might portend than in claiming a suitably large part of the action. In the buoyant atmosphere of that moment, confidence in the efficacy of American arms left little room for skepticism and doubt. As a result, senior military leaders left unasked questions of fundamental importance. What if the effect of projecting U.S. military power was not to solve problems but to exacerbate them? What if expectations of doing more with less proved hollow? What consequences would then ensue? Who would bear them?

FALSE DAWN

The answers to these questions—their very existence unacknowledged prior to 9/11—became apparent soon after President George W. Bush committed U.S. ground forces to Afghanistan and then Iraq. Granted, the army that deployed into these war zones was not Force XXI come to fruition—a full decade after Desert Storm, that concept was still more PowerPoint presentation than reality. In pursuit of a paradigm that emphasized flexibility and agility, the army had moved at a glacial pace.[45]

During the interval between Desert Storm and 9/11, outsized dreams turned out to carry outsized price tags and produced some outsized disappointments. For example, a program to develop a radar-evading helicopter, touted as "the quarterdeck of the digital battlefield," burned through $6.9 billion before being canceled.[46] The yield: two aircraft suitable for museum display. The army's Crusader artillery program, intended to produce precise, high-volume cannon fire, consumed another $2 billion prior to its 2002 termination.[47] Fort Sill, Oklahoma, provides a permanent resting place for a prototype of this forty-ton behemoth. Most ambitious of all was the army's Future Combat Systems (FCS) program, conceived in 1995 with an eye to creating a "family" of "weapons, drones, robots, sensors and hybrid-electric combat vehicles connected by a wireless network."[48] By the time FCS met its demise in 2009, the cost to the American taxpayer exceeded $18 billion.[49]

Still, the various imperatives, tenets, thrusts, objectives, and concepts conjured up to describe the army's future created expectations in the here and now. If Force XXI was missing in action, the thinking behind it—above all, the expectation that a small, nimble, "smart" force could dominate any opponent in any environment—had taken Washington's national security elite by storm.

No one believed more strongly that information technology was revolutionizing warfare than Donald Rumsfeld. When he became secretary of defense in January 2001, he was fired by the conviction that the armed forces were acting too slowly in capitalizing on this revolution. As the Pentagon's maximum leader, he aimed to fix that. The word devised to describe this project was *transformation*.[50]

The events of 9/11 provided Rumsfeld with a ready-made opportunity to advance his agenda. During the 1990s, the varied, small-scale contingencies of OOTW had kept the services busy. In terms of scope and importance, the Global War on Terrorism promised to be something altogether different. Just days after the attack on the World Trade Center and the Pentagon, the commander in chief issued the military its marching orders. "Be ready," George W. Bush said. "The hour is coming when America will act, and you will make us proud."[51] Implicit in that expression of confidence was a challenge: for the all-volunteer force, testing time had arrived.

In its own eyes, the army had been girding for just such a test throughout the previous decade. Yet despite concerted efforts to refashion itself into a war-winning power-projection force, the army did not qualify as Rumsfeld's favorite service.[52] In the secretary's eyes, words like *nimble* and *smart* conjured up images of satellite-guided air weapons delivered in support of gizmo-toting commandos. The army might talk the talk, but it didn't walk the walk. Much like the Crusader artillery system, it still came across as a lumbering behemoth—more yesterday than tomorrow. The problem, in his estimation, began at the top, the secretary of defense telling a subordinate (apparently in jest) that "lining up fifty of its generals in the Pentagon and gunning them down" would be just the thing to get the army moving in the right direction.[53]

One of those generals was Eric Shinseki. Army chief of staff in 2001, he believed that the solution to the army's Rumsfeld problem was to get with Rumsfeld's program. "If you dislike change," he warned his fellow officers, "you're going to dislike irrelevance even more."[54] But Shinseki could never convince Rumsfeld that the army was committed to transformation—perhaps because it wasn't, at least not as Rumsfeld understood the term.

Belief carries implications; the more radical the convictions, the more radical the implications. Through several decades of sustained effort, the post-Vietnam/post–Cold War army had accumulated a stock of valued possessions, regaining a sense of self-worth and restoring its standing in the eyes of the American people. As far as the generals were concerned, they had been engaged in transformation for years before Rumsfeld appropriated the term.

Now they learned that these past efforts were nowhere near good enough. In effect, the secretary of defense wanted generals like Shinseki to put those achievements at risk, following him blindly down a path toward some vastly greater treasure. This even Shinseki ultimately proved unwilling to do.

His dispute with Rumsfeld (and other proponents of radical transformation) came down to differences of opinion on the role of *quantity* in modern warfare. The army chief of staff fully endorsed the general proposition that advanced technology was making it possible to do ever more with less. Where Shinseki parted company with Rumsfeld was over the question of how much more with how much less.

To appreciate the pervasiveness of this do-more-with-less approach, compare Washington's response to 9/11 to the way it had reacted to the onset of war in 1861 or 1917 or 1941. In contrast to those other major wars, Washington embarked on the Global War on Terrorism without taking the trouble to expand its armed forces. Why bother? In terms of military capabilities, the adversary was demonstrably weak, with the enemy confronting the United States not even remotely comparable to, say, the Kaiser's Germany or the Führer's. Even after the events of 9/11, war was less a necessity than an option, even if in some quarters a welcome one.

So the nation did not mobilize. Congress did not raise taxes, curtail consumption, or otherwise adjust domestic priorities to accommodate wartime requirements. That a state undertaking what it explicitly called *global* war might consider reinstituting conscription was too far-fetched even to contemplate. The implicit assumption—shared in military and civilian quarters alike—was that existing U.S. military capacity was more than ample for the paltry tasks at hand. That the initial U.S. intervention in Afghanistan in October 2001, with a relative handful of troops and CIA agents supported by sophisticated airpower, overthrew the Taliban in a matter of weeks seemed to affirm this assumption. The implications appeared incontrovertible: the unsurpassed quality of U.S. forces made it unnecessary even to consider questions of quantity.

Shinseki, however, began to have second thoughts about this consensus. Yet when he expressed them—thereby confirming Rumsfeld's view that the army's top leaders were incorrigible—his concern was not with war's conduct but with its aftermath. In the run-up to the invasion of Iraq, the general testified before Congress that occupation was almost certain to require more U.S. troops than would conquest. Here, he predicted, was one task where the do-more-better-with-less formula was not going to apply.

Shinseki's dissent turned out to be a quixotic gesture, although earning him a humiliating rebuke, publicly administered on Rumsfeld's behalf by Deputy Secretary of Defense Paul Wolfowitz.[55] It did nothing to slow the Bush administration's rush to invade Iraq, in part because Rumsfeld didn't need the army chief of staff's consent and wasn't about to court his approval. Besides, the secretary of defense had already identified another army general willing to do his bidding. This was Tommy Franks, head of U.S. Central Command, and as such the officer immediately responsible for the ongoing war in Afghanistan and the forthcoming one in Iraq.

Whether Franks personally devised the plan for invading Iraq or whether Rumsfeld coached, cajoled, and bullied his field commander into accepting an approach incorporating his own predilections—accounts differ on how to apportion the credit (or blame) for what ensued[56]—one thing is certain. Conceptually, the operation dubbed Iraqi Freedom reflected both the ideas of those intent on refashioning the armed forces into something never before seen and the vision of a high-tech power-projection army that Sullivan and his colleagues had laid out a decade before. The media termed the result—put on vivid display as U.S. forces dashed toward Baghdad in March 2003—"shock and awe."[57]

In the wake of Saddam Hussein's overthrow, Sullivan himself wasted no time in tracing the origins of "shock and awe" back to the early 1990s. An effusive profile of Franks appearing in the *Washington Post* soon after the fall of Baghdad cited the post–Desert Storm period as a turning point in his career. At the time, the *Post* reported, General Sullivan "was eager to move the Army fully into computerized, technological warfare." But as army chief of staff, he needed help. "I was looking for an imaginative and creative guy," Sullivan recalled. "Tommy was the guy I went to." Sullivan paid tribute to the victorious Franks as "one of the architects" of a revolutionary new American way of war.[58]

In his own account, Franks went considerably farther. Not content to be one architect among several, he claimed exclusive credit for engineering "a true revolution in warfare." That quality trumped quantity in modern combat rated as his own personal discovery. "We would not apply overwhelming force," he wrote in describing his thinking about how to attack Iraq. "Rather, we would apply the overwhelming 'mass effect' of a smaller force. Speed would represent a mass all its own." Information technology—better intelligence, more flexible command and control, precision weapons, and just-in-time logistics—made such greater speed possible. Franks was adamant in insisting that his thinking represented "a revolutionary concept, way outside the box of conventional doctrine."[59] The implications were self-evident: you didn't need a big army to do big things.

Yet Franks erred on two counts. His lesser error was to claim more credit than was his due. In fact, his "revolutionary concept" recycled the very same clichés that generals had been reciting ever since Operation Desert Storm. His greater error was to insist that his revolutionary concept had, indeed, yielded a historic triumph, satisfying the standard that Sullivan had set a decade earlier: decisive victory achieved with a "minimal expenditure of national wealth and resources."

The first error—unseemly braggadocio—spoke ill of the man. The second error, which ultimately proved fatal to Franks's reputation (and Rumsfeld's), had far more significant implications for the army and the United States. Rather than marking the end of a short war, the overthrow of Saddam Hussein inaugurated a long one. In contrast to 73 Easting, when *this* fight appeared over, it had barely begun. Faced with challenges that Franks had failed to anticipate and for which his soldiers were ill-prepared, the power-projection army sent to "liberate" Iraq became perforce an army of occupation engaged in imperial policing. The ensuing struggle consumed wealth (increasingly borrowed from abroad) and resources (lives lost and damaged) on an epic scale. America, Sullivan had written in 1992, "does not expect protracted, attrition warfare."[60] Barely more than a decade later, that's precisely what it got.

Or more precisely still, that's what the army (and Marine Corps) got. Who exactly U.S. troops were fighting in Iraq was never entirely clear. The enemy manifested about as much political cohesion and unity of effort as the Native American tribes that the United States Army had labored to pacify through much of the nineteenth century. Yet the absence of apparent unity did not make the various Sunni and Shiite factions, reinforced by "foreign fighters," any less formidable. Indeed, the insurgents provided U.S. troops with an object lesson in how combatants actually *could* do more with less: relying on crude, locally fabricated mines—Improvised Explosive Devices (IEDs), the Americans called them—they gave expensively equipped, high-tech U.S. forces fits. The Pentagon had confused sophistication with cost. Iraq's insurgents did not make the same mistake.

As the war dragged on, it prompted division on the home front without fully engaging the attention and energy of the American people. Many millions supported the war, while suppressing any urge to deliver their military-age offspring into the waiting hands of the nearest recruiter. Millions more reviled the war, yet expressions of opposition were muted. Protests occurred, but in scope and intensity antiwar activism paled in comparison to what had occurred during the Vietnam War. On one point only the war's supporters and the war's opponents agreed with near unanimity: whatever the course of events in Iraq, professing support for America's "warriors" remained a categorical imperative.

7

COPING WITH CHAOS

The victory to which Franks laid claim proved to be a chimera. If technology was changing the nature of warfare in ways that conferred advantages on U.S. forces, someone had forgotten to tell the insurgents. In Iraq, the enemy (or enemies) recovered, regrouped, continued to fight. According to army doctrine, winning the first battle held the key to winning any war. This chestnut to which the post–Cold War officer corps was deeply devoted turned out to be false. Iraq soon descended into chaos, with soldiers left holding the bag.

As it became apparent that nothing remotely like victory was in the offing, army leaders found themselves facing an uncomfortable question: what exactly had gone wrong? With striking alacrity, they let themselves off the hook. Training their guns on Rumsfeld, they saddled him with the blame, while for whatever reason giving his boss a pass. A veritable "revolt of the generals" erupted as just-retired senior officers took turns lambasting the secretary of defense in print and on the airwaves.[1] A *New York Times* op-ed by retired Major General Paul Eaton was typical, blasting Rumsfeld as "not competent to lead our armed forces." In ticking off Rumsfeld's failings, Eaton singled out "his unrealistic confidence in technology to replace manpower," along with his failure to "understand the nature of protracted counterinsurgency warfare in Iraq and the demands it places on ground forces."[2]

Yet the post–Cold War army in which Eaton had served fully shared in the expectation that technology could indeed replace manpower. Similarly, that army had paid little if any attention to the problems posed by counterinsurgency. An army confident that it had discovered a surefire formula all but guaranteeing outright victory was no more inclined to worry about irregular warfare than to practice conducting a retreat.

In lieu of decisive victory, committing the power-projection military to Iraq (and Afghanistan) triggered a cascade of ill effects. The active duty force turned out to be not only smaller than it had been during the Cold War but much too small for the tasks at hand. The quality differential—highly trained, extravagantly equipped troops—did not fully compensate for the shortage of numbers.

Given the reliance on volunteers—more broadly, given the fact that military service had become a matter of choice rather than obligation—there existed no easy way to convert a too-small force into a sufficiently large one. Material inducements (pay raises and enlistment bonuses) came with a hefty price tag. So, too, did marketing, with the Pentagon's promotional budget for 2012 reaching a cool $667 million.[3] Although some potential recruits responded to psychic inducements—patriotism or a yearning to "be part of something bigger than yourself"—the appeal of military service during wartime remained limited. In a 2012 survey of America's "ten worst jobs," for example, respondents rated soldiering number three.[4]

For career regulars, all this translated into recurring combat tours. A year in the war zone followed by a year at home followed by orders back to war—for active duty soldiers, this became the new normal. Sullivan's vision of an army that would "do it over and over again, allowing him no time to react, recover, or regroup," had achieved an ironic fulfillment. Yet the *him* subjected to recurring punishment turned out to be not the enemy but the individual American soldier. In contrast to Vietnam, the army as a whole did not disintegrate, nor did troops in the ranks protest or revolt. They kept going back again and again to wars they could not win. As it turned out, the hallmark of Abe's army was not that it excelled at achieving victory, but that it possessed an astonishing capacity just to keep at it.

Yet the effects of multiple combat tours ranged from troubling to downright horrifying. Troops beset with demons turned increasingly to alcohol and drugs.[5] Official policy all but endorsed this tendency. In 2011, the year the Iraq War ended, one out of every five active duty soldiers was on antidepressants, sedatives, or other prescription drugs.[6] The incidence of spousal abuse spiked, as did the divorce rate among military couples.[7] Debilitating combat stress reached epidemic proportions.[8] So did brain injuries.[9] Soldier suicides skyrocketed.[10]

In an effort to narrow the gap between too much war and too few soldiers—itself rooted in the gap separating the military from society—army leaders called increasingly upon reservists and members of the National Guard, many of whom were activated for multiple combat tours. The military thereby voided the implicit contract that had defined the terms of service for these part-time soldiers—that the nation would call upon them only in extreme emergencies—and converted them in effect into an adjunct of the active-duty force.[11] Here, too, pathologies stemming from exposure to combat—compounded by recurrent disruptions of personal life—exacted their toll.

The conversion of reservists into quasi professionals was not without irony. After the Vietnam War, Creighton Abrams had counted on the reserves—the last remnant of the citizen-soldier tradition—to shield the regular army from misuse by feckless policy makers. By making the active-duty army dependent on the reserves for certain essential support functions, he sought to preclude Washington from waging large-scale war without first making the politically difficult decision to mobilize. He meant, in other words, to give decision makers pause.[12] It hadn't worked out that way, however. Instead, in the wake of 9/11, the reserves took their place in a rotation scheme devised to sustain just the sort of protracted conflict Abrams had been intent on avoiding.

In addition, fielding an army of professionals in wartime turned out to be an exceedingly expensive proposition. Initially justified in part to save money—"the cost of a volunteer army, properly calculated, [will] almost surely be less than of a conscripted army," the economist Milton Friedman had promised back in 1966—the all-volunteer force actually turned out to be a dubious bargain.[13] By 2012, the monthly salary of a private first class had risen to a hardly munificent $1,757. Yet to maintain each and every soldier that the United States deployed to war zones such as Iraq and Afghanistan, the army was spending a million dollars per year.[14]

Then there were the downstream costs. Although not easily calculated, the expenses associated with caring for veterans of Iraq, Afghanistan, and other lesser contingencies promised to be off the charts. Among the leading indicators: since 2000, disability benefits paid to U.S. veterans have nearly quadrupled, from $15 billion to $57 billion per year. Already a quarter of the approximately 2.3 million Iraq and Afghanistan War veterans have claimed a service-connected disability—a figure sure to grow as the population ages.[15] Given that veterans' claims do not reach their peak until thirty to forty years after a conflict, costs will surely rise further. One analyst estimates that when the last bill comes due decades from now, total veterans' disability claims stemming from the "long wars" of the early twenty-first century will approach $1 trillion.[16]

THE REDEEMER COMETH

For soldiers deploying on repetitive combat tours, service in Iraq became a recurring Golgotha, events there laying bare the shortcomings of Sullivan's formula for "land power dominance." (As long as the Iraq War claimed priority attention, Afghanistan barely qualified as an afterthought.) With the passage of time, civilian and military leaders ratcheted down expectations of what U.S. forces could achieve in Iraq. Whatever the actual aim, it wasn't victory. In late 2006, President George W. Bush made this official, firing Rumsfeld and handing responsibility for the war's conduct to a new field commander, General David Petraeus, who prudently avoided rash promises of defeating the insurgency outright. His stated aim was considerably more modest: "to achieve sufficient security to provide the space and time for the Iraqi government to come to grips with the tough decisions its members must make to enable Iraq to move forward."[17] To turn things around, Petraeus proposed to apply the precepts of counterinsurgency, or COIN, as it was known among enthusiasts.[18]

During the year prior to Petraeus's appointment, this new approach—which in U.S. military circles wasn't so much new as forgotten—had received a preliminary test run. In the city of Tal Afar, H. R. McMaster, the hero of 73 Easting, now a colonel commanding an armored cavalry regiment, had implemented the methods that Petraeus proposed to apply across Iraq.[19] Patience and careful calculation—not speed and technology—enabled a very astute commander to restore a semblance of security and of normalcy to one Iraqi city. Now another astute—and politically savvy—commander set out to replicate that achievement on a far broader scale.

The campaign that followed—popularly known as "the surge" because the total number of U.S. troops in Iraq temporarily increased—did avert unmitigated defeat. Violence in Iraq subsided, albeit for reasons that remain in dispute.[20] Yet the judgment of enthusiasts that the surge "easily bears comparison with Patton's race across France or the Soviet destruction of German forces in 1944 and 1945" is unlikely to stand, if only because the results achieved proved so much less than definitive.[21] Even after U.S. commanders declared the surge a success, the insurgency in Iraq persisted—indeed, does so today with attacks and bombings in Baghdad and other cities (including Tal Afar) still commonplace.[22]

More to the point, by embracing COIN as its new MO, the army in effect abrogated its claim to deliver swift and economical results. Counterinsurgency was "shock and awe" inverted—not quick, not cheap, and seldom conclusive. As such, it proved a hard sell to political leaders and citizens not known for their patience. On one point Sullivan had been right: his countrymen didn't cotton to protracted, attrition warfare. So although Americans might admire Colonel McMaster's achievements at Tal Afar, Captain McMaster's heroics at 73 Easting were more to their liking, and what army leaders had led them to expect.

Petraeus offered deliverance of a sort—he "exemplified the Army finally getting it right in Iraq," one officer observed—thereby facilitating its escape from Golgotha.[23] Yet COIN could not provide a lasting remedy for the collapse of institutional purpose in Iraq. For the best army in the world, "getting it right" was not the same as winning.

The army's predicament midway in the Iraq War could be

compared to that of the battleship navy after Pearl Harbor. Soften-
ing up enemy-occupied islands in the Pacific might qualify as
honorable employment, but it was a far cry from what these ships
had been designed to do: sink the enemy's battle fleet. To be consigned to a supporting role was slightly embarrassing and left the
battleship's future looking dim.

So even granting the extravagant claims made by those liken-
ing Petraeus to Patton or ascribing to him the qualities of a "mav-
erick savior," the surge posed a problem.[24] If its "success" in Iraq
defined the army's principal contribution to national security, the
service was in trouble.

Indeed, when General Stanley McChrystal's attempt to export
COIN to Afghanistan in 2009–10 fizzled, the counterinsurgency
balloon quickly deflated. By 2012, the doctrine that Petraeus
(drawing on the achievements of Colonel McMaster) had made his
name promoting was just as dead as the power-projection doctrine
Sullivan (inspired by the achievements of Captain McMaster)
had inaugurated twenty years earlier.

If doubts remained, President Barack Obama removed them.
His administration wasn't giving up on power projection per se.
His affinity for drone strikes, commando raids, and cyberattacks
made that clear enough. Yet Bush's successor had little appetite for
starting new large-scale land wars. On that score Robert Gates,
Rumsfeld's successor as secretary of defense (retained by Obama),
had made the definitive statement, telling the Corps of Cadets at
West Point that "any future defense secretary who advises the
president to again send a big American land army into Asia or into
the Middle East or Africa should 'have his head examined,' as
General MacArthur so delicately put it."[25] Gates no doubt intended
this to be a headline-grabbing sound bite, and so it proved.

Unreconstructed hawks objected, of course. In the *Weekly Standard*, William Kristol found Gates guilty of failing to understand

"that American power is a crucial force for good in the world" and charged him with "undercutting" the troops.[26] Still, in expressing an aversion to further invasions in the Greater Middle East, Gates accurately gauged the country's prevailing mood. Generals like Gordon Sullivan could hardly interpret the secretary's comment as anything other than a backhanded rebuke.

QUESTIONS OF PURPOSE

The serial disappointments of Iraq and Afghanistan—the two longest wars in U.S. history—had surprisingly little effect on the army's overall standing in the eyes of the American people and American elites. An attitude of cordial indifference—akin perhaps to the way that most nonbelievers view the Sunday morning rituals of churchgoers—continued to prevail. Yet after more than a decade of continuous combat, what exactly did this army exist to do, either in its own eyes or in the nation's?

A new generation of senior leaders stuck to the old script: the army exists to fight and win the nation's wars, they insisted. With a fervor matching Gordon Sullivan's two decades prior, they reasserted his single standard of success: clear-cut, unambiguous victory. Choosing his words with exquisite care, army chief of staff General Raymond Odierno told Congress in 2012 that his service had "successfully concluded" its operations in Iraq while efforts to "transfer security responsibilities" in Afghanistan were ongoing. Having avoided any mention of the V-word, he then unblushingly described the army as the "nation's force of decisive action" ready to win any war "decisively and dominantly."[27] Army General Martin Dempsey, then chairman of the Joint Chiefs of Staff, echoed these views. With the Pentagon facing the possibility of modest cuts in the overall size of U.S. forces, he insisted that the country possessed "a military that can win any conflict, anywhere." Reiterating a theme that Sullivan had once propounded, he stubbornly avowed that "capability is more important than size."[28]

Yet the army had emphatically *not* won the conflicts in which Odierno and Dempsey had recently participated. In truth, since 1945 the U.S. Army has not achieved anything approximating victory in any contest larger than policing exercises like the 1983 intervention in Grenada or the 1990 invasion of Panama. The army in which Odierno and Dempsey had ascended to the top could win battles, of that there was little doubt. Yet its ability to achieve real success in any war worthy of the name was subject to considerable question. At the end of the day, it's outcomes that count, and the American army had struggled mightily to deliver the outcomes promised.[29]

In the spring of 2012, Colonel Gregory A. Daddis, a historian teaching at West Point, conceded, "We're not really sure right now what the Army is for."[30] Here was candor rare among serving officers and virtually nonexistent at the three- and four-star level. In the navy, the air force, and the Marine Corps, no such existential confusion existed.

At roughly the same time, H. R. McMaster, by now a highly regarded major general charged with rooting out corruption in the Afghan government, commented in an interview with the *Wall Street Journal*, "We have a perfect record in predicting future wars—right? . . . And that record is 0%." Yet despite this unerring appraisal of an unerringly dismal record, he found reason to take heart. "The story that will be told years from now," McMaster continued, "is one of adaptability to mission sets and circumstances that were not clearly defined or anticipated prior to those wars."[31] Yet as both Afghanistan and Iraq had demonstrated, adaptability is anything but synonymous with mission accomplishment, which had become difficult even to define. As a warrior-turned-anticorruption-czar, General McMaster personified the army's adaptability. Still, by the time he completed his tour of duty in Afghanistan, had McMaster's efforts to reduce official corruption there succeeded? By what standard? And why, apart from his availability, did it make sense to assign this chore to an American military officer? Merely to pose such questions provided one measure of the journey that McMaster's army had taken since the heady days of 73 Easting.

The impulse to refashion the army into an instrument of global interventionism for use in places like Iraq and Afghanistan had not originated with Donald Rumsfeld nor with any of his immediate predecessors as secretary of defense. Acting on their own volition, army leaders had chosen that course. Disregarding the Cold War's central military lesson—that land power is most effective when employed to deter and defend—generals dazzled by Operation Desert Storm eagerly embraced the proposition that the active employment of military power offered an attractive way to alleviate the world's ailments. That the smaller post–Cold War army might have been better off attempting less with less—an appreciation of the risks and uncertainties inherent in war promoting an attitude of modesty and caution—received no consideration whatsoever. Neither did the possibility that such an approach might better serve the nation that the generals had sworn to defend while preserving from unnecessary harm the soldiers they professed to love.

PART III

SKIN IN THE GAME

How politicians, military officers, and intellectuals, helped by a compliant citizenry, collaborate to avoid unwelcome truths about the failing American way of war.

8

SMEDLEY AND FRIENDS

Call it Smedley's syndrome: a senior U.S. military officer in retirement defects and thereby makes headlines. In doing so, he commits a kind of treason in the second degree, not betraying his country but calling into question officially sanctioned truths. After decades of unquestioning subservience to the national security state, he aligns himself with crazies and wackos, lending credence to views hitherto classified as disreputable, outlandish, or at the very least heretical.

Marine Major General Smedley Butler, the syndrome's progenitor, achieved notoriety by announcing immediately upon his departure from active duty in 1933 that he had spent the previous several decades "being a high class muscle-man for Big Business, for Wall Street and for the Bankers. In short, I was a racketeer, a gangster for capitalism." In left-wing circles, the general instantly ascended to the status of folk hero. Critics of U.S. policy welcomed with enthusiasm his admission that venality, not high ideals, had prompted Washington, acting at the behest of the moneyed classes, to intervene militarily in China, Mexico, and throughout the

Caribbean (not to mention France in 1917). As for why the truth had for so long eluded him, they readily accepted Butler's self-exculpatory explanation. "I never had a thought of my own until I left the service," the general confessed. As a dutiful agent of a deeply corrupt enterprise, his "mental faculties [had] remained in suspended animation," a condition he described as "typical with everyone in the military service."[1] In antiwar circles, Smedley Butler remains even today a celebrated figure, a blunt teller of truths.

Six decades later, General Lee Butler (no relation to Smedley) offered yet another case in which a senior officer's retirement from active duty inspired a sudden outburst of candor. An air force officer, Butler spent his career as a nuclear weapons specialist. During his rise to four-star rank culminating in his assignment as head of U.S. Strategic Command, he was by his own account "embroiled in every aspect of American nuclear policymaking and force posturing, from the councils of government to military command centers, from cramped bomber cockpits to the suffocating confines of ballistic missile submarines." Butler "certified hundreds of crews for their nuclear mission and approved thousands of targets for potential nuclear destruction." Here was a flesh-and-blood, if far less colorful, equivalent of Stanley Kubrick's General Buck Turgidson, dedicated to the proposition that standing in readiness to blow up the planet held the key to keeping the peace. During the Cold War, antinuclear crusaders had denounced such thinking as madness. Air force officers had dismissed such criticism as naive.

Yet no sooner did Butler retire in 1994 than he switched sides, characterizing nuclear weapons as "inherently dangerous, hugely expensive, militarily inefficient and morally indefensible" and nuclear war as "a raging, insatiable beast whose instincts and appetites we pretend to understand but cannot possibly control"—just what the peaceniks had been saying all along.[2] The U.S. nuclear arsenal had not deterred the Soviet Union, he insisted; instead the "presence of these hideous devices unnecessarily prolonged and intensified the Cold War."[3] As with Smedley Butler, the cause to which Lee Butler had devoted his professional life turned out—so he belatedly discovered—to have been false.

Some officers suffer the onset of Smedley's syndrome only after a considerable lapse of time. Admiral William H. Standley offers an example. Prior to World War II, President Franklin D. Roosevelt had appointed Standley to the position of chief of naval operations, the U.S. Navy's top post. During the war, Roosevelt sent him to Moscow, where the admiral did a tour as U.S. ambassador. In between those two assignments, he served on the Roberts Commission, created in mid-December 1941 to investigate the Japanese attack on Pearl Harbor.

The commission's purpose was to fix accountability for this disaster. Its hastily drafted report did just that, charging the senior army and navy commanders in Hawaii with "dereliction of duty."[4] As a consequence, Admiral Husband Kimmel and Lieutenant General Walter Short lost their jobs; the people to whom Kimmel and Short reported and from whom they got their marching orders kept theirs. Standley and his colleagues concurred unanimously in the report's findings.

Yet the commission's narrowly drawn conclusions almost immediately fueled suspicions of a whitewash—suspicions that Standley himself ultimately endorsed. As with the Generals Butler, so, too, with Admiral Standley: the transition from insider to outsider gave rise to second thoughts. In 1954, he denounced the Roberts Commission's findings, stating his "firm belief that the real responsibility for the disaster at Pearl Harbor was lodged thousands of miles from the Territory of Hawaii." Kimmel and Short had been "martyred." A fair-minded investigation would have found the uniformed heads of the army and navy back in Washington "fully culpable." The whole purpose of the "hurriedly

ordered" Roberts Commission, he now declared, had been "to fore-
stall" any congressional inclination to ask unwelcome questions.

And plenty of questions needed asking. Standley hinted that
members of Roosevelt's inner circle had welcomed—and even
facilitated—the events of December 7. "The 'incident' which certain high officials in Washington had sought so assiduously in
order to condition the American public for war with the Axis
powers had been found." None of Standley's charges were novel;
yet coming from a former four-star admiral who in 1942 helped
draft the Roberts Commission's report, they represented a striking
about-face.[5]

The case of Admiral Thomas Moorer followed a similar pattern, although with a longer gestation period. Just weeks before
Moorer assumed office as chief of naval operations in midsum-
mer 1967, his service had sustained its most devastating attack
since World War II. On June 8, Israeli naval and air forces bombed,
strafed, and torpedoed the USS *Liberty*, an intelligence collection
ship sailing in international waters off the coast of Egypt.
Although the attackers did not succeed in sinking the *Liberty*,
they inflicted considerable damage, killing 34 Americans and
wounding another 171.

Ascribing the incident to a case of mistaken identity, the government of Israel quickly apologized. After a perfunctory court
of inquiry, the navy—and by extension the U.S. government—
accepted the Israeli explanation. Moorer himself signed off on the
court's findings, which neatly meshed with the preferences of
President Lyndon Johnson.[6] Yet as with the Roberts Commission
report, the conclusions that the navy reached with such alacrity
served to enflame rather than ease suspicions that all was not
kosher. Critics cried cover-up, insisting that Israel had deliberately
attacked the *Liberty*, knowing full well that it was an American
vessel, but determined to prevent it from eavesdropping on Israeli

military operations. Like Pearl Harbor itself (not to mention the assassination of John F. Kennedy, the events of 9/11, and questions about Barack Obama's birthplace), official explanations intended to suppress doubts exacerbated them. The issue festered.

After keeping silent for several decades, Moorer himself suddenly felt compelled to weigh in. In 2003, he went public, charging Israel with "acts of murder against American servicemen and an act of war against the United States." More remarkably, in keeping with the tradition of Smedley Butler, Moorer accused the service that he had led with orchestrating "an official cover-up without precedent in American naval history."[7]

Why hadn't either of the Generals Butler expressed their concerns about U.S. policy when they were occupying positions of influence? Why, in the face of perceived injustice or duplicity, did Admirals Standley and Moorer keep mum, speaking up only long after the fact? The elder Butler's claim of being incapable of independent thought while in uniform conforms to a civilian stereotype of obedient, brain-dead soldiers, but won't do. Prolonged immersion in the military bureaucracy may impair, but need not eradicate, critical judgment. A more accurate explanation would perhaps go like this: for some senior officers—just as for others engaged in pursuits where upward mobility provides the principal measure of merit—departure from that environment modifies the hierarchy of interests to which they had reflexively subscribed. When getting ahead and wielding authority no longer take precedence over all other considerations, the moral landscape can take on a different appearance.[8]

So for a handful of senior officers, the very act of stepping down from the heights of their profession may have the paradoxical effect of expanding their horizons. For the likes of Admirals Standley or Moorer, judgments that once appeared necessary or at least expedient became unconscionable. For the Generals Butler, basic policies once considered sacrosanct suddenly seemed beyond the pale.

GOING ROGUE

Such apparently has been the case with General Stanley McChrystal, the most recent senior officer to exhibit symptoms of Smedley's syndrome. The episodes cited above qualify as historical curiosities. The McChrystal case is different. It illuminates the dysfunctional nature of the present-day relationship between the U.S. military and American society, while hinting at why this relationship persists and will in all likelihood continue to do so.

A professional soldier who spent most of his career in the "black" world of special operations forces, McChrystal first came to public attention in 2009 when President Barack Obama appointed him commander of all U.S. and NATO forces in Afghanistan. As a candidate for president, Obama had vowed to reinvigorate the war effort there, after years during which Iraq had claimed the preponderance of resources and attention. His appointment of the hard-charging McChrystal symbolized his intention to make good on that promise.

Just as the new president's election had generated media-hyped expectations of big change, so McChrystal's arrival in Kabul seemed to herald the prospect of the war there dramatically turning around. To Afghanistan, McChrystal was bringing methods General David Petraeus had employed in Iraq. Given that he had worked closely with Petraeus in Iraq, McChrystal seemed like precisely the right guy to achieve similarly happy results in Afghanistan, a latter-day Francis Xavier continuing the work begun by Ignatius Loyola.

Unfortunately, events soon exposed as false the premises underlying those expectations. The Afghanistan War no more resembled the Iraq War than baseball resembles basketball. To imagine that techniques employed in one war will automatically apply to another was naive in the extreme. As McChrystal himself acknowledged in retrospect, his grasp of the challenges he faced in Afghanistan was remarkably shallow. "We didn't know enough and we still don't know enough," he conceded. "Most of us—me included—had a very superficial understanding of the situation and history, and we had a frighteningly simplistic view of recent history, the last 50 years."[9]

Worse yet, when it came to observing the formalities of civilian control, the general turned out to be either spectacularly arrogant or stunningly obtuse. His expansive definition of his own authority—he acted as if President Obama's job was simply to concur with whatever his field commander might decide—encroached on the prerogatives of the commander in chief. Meanwhile, McChrystal's headquarters had become a sort of petri dish of rancor and resentment directed at ostensibly clueless politicians said to impede the efforts of seasoned warriors who knew exactly what needed to be done.

In the end, McChrystal lasted about a year in the job. A much-publicized magazine article that depicted him as finding nothing amiss while his closest subordinates ridiculed senior civilian officials in his presence provided the proximate cause for his ouster.[10] As the general departed Afghanistan, little evidence existed to suggest that the war's momentum had shifted. The latter-day Francis Xavier's efforts to convert the heathen had fallen flat.

Not for McChrystal, however, the hoary dictum calling on old soldiers to fade quietly away. Not long after being hustled into retirement, he began to opine on basic national security policy. Yet rather than denouncing muckraking journalists (who embarrass generals) or meddling politicians (who stick their noses into soldiers' business), he chose as his primary target that most sacred of post-Vietnam military cows: the all-volunteer force.

"I think we ought to have a draft," McChrystal told a rapt audience gathered for the 2012 Aspen Ideas Festival. Because a professional military necessarily becomes "unrepresentative of the population," it cannot properly represent the country as a whole. "I think if a nation goes to war," he continued, "every town, every city needs to be at risk." Only then will everyone have "skin in the game." Here was the equivalent of a cardinal archbishop of the Catholic Church declaring obsolete the tradition of an all-male, celibate priesthood. Smedley's syndrome had evidently claimed another victim.[11]

Expecting a small force of regulars to bear the burden of protracted conflict, he insisted, was unfair and un-American. "We've never done that in the United States before; we've never fought an extended war with an all-volunteer military. So what it means is you've got a very small population that you're going to and you're going to it over and over again." With "less than one percent of the population" in uniform, Americans may purport to be supportive, "but they don't have the same connection" with the professional army they had with the citizen-soldier army of earlier days. "I've enjoyed the benefits of a professional service, but I think we'd be better if we actually went to a draft these days," McChrystal concluded, thereby committing sacrilege akin to Smedley Butler decrying American imperialism and Lee Butler denouncing nuclear weapons as immoral. "There would be some loss of professionalism, but for the nation it would be a better course."[12]

McChrystal did not specifically identify the "benefits of a professional service" that he had enjoyed, nor did he question the wisdom of the United States engaging in "extended war," as it had been doing for more than a decade. Instead, striking a position that was simultaneously radical and retrograde, he merely questioned whether relying on regulars to wage America's wars could possibly be right given that the vast majority of citizens thereby had no immediate stake in the enterprise.

Initially sold as a solution to problems, the all-volunteer force, McChrystal implied, had become the problem. Abandoned during the Vietnam era as unfair and at odds with maintaining good order and discipline, conscription now held the key to restoring a sense of equity when it came to military service and sacrifice.

Others had been making this point long before McChrystal spoke, just as others had questioned official accounts of the attack on Pearl Harbor and the assault on the USS *Liberty*, long before Admirals Standley and Moorer offered their dissents. As someone who has discussed U.S. military policy with dozens of audiences over the past decade, I can count on one hand the number of occasions when someone did *not* pose a question about the draft, invariably offered as a suggestion for how to curb Washington's appetite for intervention abroad and establish some semblance of political accountability.

McChrystal's call for restoring conscription and by implication reviving the citizen-soldier tradition endowed a hitherto quirky view with a tincture of legitimacy. Yet this retired general's belated appreciation of citizen-soldiers is no more likely to inspire a change in policy than did the belated discovery by earlier retired generals that imperialism is as American as apple pie or that a security policy based on nuclear weapons ultimately produces insecurity and daunting moral snares. The more pressing question is one to which even now McChrystal seemingly remains oblivious: what exactly is the "game" and who are its beneficiaries?

9

WINNERS AND LOSERS

McChrystal's critique of the all-volunteer force will go unheeded for one overriding reason: existing arrangements satisfy the interests and advance the ambitions of those who wield (or covet) power. In that regard, the all-volunteer force resembles academic tenure. Arguments presented by proponents—defenders of America's professionalized military touting its value in advancing the cause of peace and security; defenders of tenure touting its value in protecting academic freedom and facilitating the pursuit of truth—tell only half the tale. Even if seldom acknowledged, the other (self-serving) half is at least as important. Tenure offers near-ironclad guarantees of lifetime employment, something that very few Americans, subject to the vagaries of the market, enjoy. Reliance on an all-volunteer force likewise suits a long list of beneficiaries. For those who ride the gravy train, doing what's necessary to keep it rolling takes precedence over contemplating its ultimate destination or the wreckage left in its wake.

The reliance on a small professional warrior class with which McChrystal now finds fault has created winners and losers. Among the big winners, united in their enthusiasm for maintaining the all-volunteer force, are the individuals, groups, and institutions comprising the national security state. These include generals, admirals, and civilian officials who fill the upper echelons of the Pentagon, the State Department, and the National Security Council staff; champions of an imperial presidency, who reflexively support anything that enhances the freedom of action exercised by the chief executive; and advocates of global interventionism, however lofty or low the ostensible motive for action.

For those enjoying access to rarified policy circles, intently surveying the globe in search of anything remotely resembling a nail, the all-volunteer force provides the proverbial hammer.[1] In the eyes of those who formulate policy or aspirants maneuvering for a chance to do so, the professional military by its very existence enriches the list of conceivable policy alternatives.

The signature phrase of contemporary American statecraft— "all options remain on the table"—derives its potency from the implied threat of military power, like some avenging angel, instantly available to back up Washington's demands. All it takes to bomb Belgrade, invade Iraq, or send Navy SEALs into Pakistan is concurrence among a half dozen people and a nod from the president. No need to secure prior congressional assent, certainly no need to consult the American people: that's what the all-volunteer force allows. For those attending that meeting-of-the-half-dozen or angling to advise some future emperor-president, the "game" is the exercise of power and the illusion of shaping history.

The now iconic photograph of President Obama and his closest associates watching in real time the raid that killed Osama bin Laden makes the point. The photo exudes immediacy, intimacy, and above all importance. This small group operating behind closed doors in Washington had rendered its decision; as an immediate consequence, a hardly larger group of Navy SEALs was executing a daring covert operation on the other side of the world. An elite that conferred in secret was directing an elite that operates in secret—with Americans offered a tiny, alluring, carefully selected, after-the-fact glimpse of what had occurred. The last thing the players in this game want is to invite popular participation. A military consisting of citizen-soldiers might lead members of the great unwashed to fancy they should have some say in such matters. Relying on warrior professionals—now embodied by the celebrated SEALs—makes it easier to deflect any such demand.[2]

Chalk it up as a posthumous victory for President Nixon. His political opponents despised Nixon's penchant for operating behind closed doors while relying on a small circle of handpicked loyalists to enforce his will. Critics (rightly) saw this as part and parcel of a larger proclivity for skullduggery and dirty tricks. Such secrecy, they insisted, was at odds with accountability. Today, when it comes to national security policy, methods that got Nixon impeached have become the norm. To a very considerable extent, Americans know only what the government wishes them to know. The professional military that Nixon played such a role in creating helps make this possible.

Yet the roster of those who benefit from the all-volunteer force extends well beyond the world of policy players and wannabes. It also includes arms manufacturers, along with those members of Congress who tend to their concerns and count on corporate generosity to keep campaign coffers brimming.[3] Then there are private security contractors (PSCs), aka mercenaries or war profiteers, engaged in the lucrative business of supplementing and supporting overextended U.S. forces in the field. For those with an eye for the main chance, the professional military is not so much a hammer as a cornucopia—a source of perpetual largesse, translating into robust profits, good-paying jobs for constituents, and by extension political advantage.[4] Here the "game" is money and the influence that money buys.

In place of the defunct collaboration between the army and the people, the Pentagon now partners with profit-motivated corporations. In deciding that a post–Cold War army could do more with less, senior leaders had, wittingly or not, opened the door to an expanded contractor presence, which soon enough translated into a veritable contractor dependency.

When post-9/11 wars expected to be very short turned out to be very long, contractors lined up at that door to claim the boodle on the other side. Soldiers had once viewed the battlefield as their exclusive jurisdiction. Now they learned to share it with the likes of KBR, DynCorp, Engility (formerly L-3 MPRI), and Academi (formerly Xe, previously Blackwater USA), hired to perform security, training, and logistics functions over which the military itself had once exercised responsibility.[5] As a consequence, the Pentagon today funnels billions of dollars to the PSCs, more than a few of them created or run by former senior military officers.[6] (Those not interested in full-time employment can rake in plenty of dough by serving PSCs as "consultants" or "strategic advisers.")[7]

In Iraq and Afghanistan, a relative handful of well-connected contractors have claimed a lion's share of the profits. As measured by dollar value, U.S. government agencies awarded over 50 percent of their contracts in war zones to a mere twenty-two firms, each of them enjoying revenues of more than $1 billion. KBR led the pack, laying claim to some $40.8 billion in contracts during the decade after 9/11.[8]

As of 2010, contractors operating in Iraq and Afghanistan had some 260,000 employees on their payrolls—more than the total number of U.S. troops committed to those theaters. Here was a government-funded "job creation" program of sizable proportions, although the vast majority of those employed were foreign nationals, not Americans. In fact, contracting actually amounted to little more than an expensive approach to concealing war's actual costs. One U.S. government study declared bluntly that contracting activities in Iraq and Afghanistan over a period of years had "entailed vast amounts of spending for little or no benefit."[9]

Evidence of contractor malfeasance gave rise to occasional tut-tutting in Congress and the media. In 2011, government investigators determined that "war planners have wasted as much as $60 billion on contract fraud and abuse in Iraq and Afghanistan, about $1 for every $3.50 spent on contractors in those countries over the last decade."[10] In other words, losses amounted to something on the order of "$12 million every day for the past ten years." In fact, such figures almost certainly understate actual losses, perhaps by orders of magnitude. The government's Commission on Wartime Contracting in Iraq and Afghanistan admitted that the "backlog of unaudited incurred costs" was on track to exceed $1 trillion by 2016.[11]

The contractor phenomenon has spawned a substantial literature from which four overarching themes emerge: among PSCs, mission performance tends to be mixed, ethical standards flexible, government oversight ineffectual, and, most of all, profit potential eye-watering.[12] Were the United States to revert to a more easily expansible, citizen-based army, PSCs would become largely redundant. As in earlier days, the Pentagon could then do for itself many of the things that it is now contracting with others to do, such as guarding its own gates, hauling its own fuel and supplies, preparing its own rations, and disposing of its own human waste, not to mention doing its own thinking. It might even revert to the practice of writing its own doctrine, rather than relying, as it has in recent years, on civilian contractors to do so. By way of example, to draft Field Manual 100-21, *Contractors on the Battlefield*, the army hired Military Professional Resources, Inc., a firm founded by retired senior army officers and itself the recipient of various contracts in Iraq and Afghanistan.[13]

As a practical matter, however, few in Washington have shown any inclination to correct this problem. Wherever the contractor goose travels, it leaves behind a trail of excrement. Yet given that the goose reliably produces such a bountiful supply of golden eggs, no one in a position of influence finds all that much cause to complain.

BURIED FOOTNOTE

Influence peddling and legally sanctioned corruption of this sort are, of course, hardly new. More than three-quarters of a century ago, a Senate investigation found that collusion between companies profiting from war and government officials "constitutes an unhealthy alliance" that "operates in the name of patriotism and satisfies interests which are, in large part, purely selfish." With considerable understatement, the Special Committee on Investigation of the Munitions Industry, also known as the Nye Committee, noted that weapons manufacturers "with competitive bribes ready in outstretched hands" had created a situation where officials become less "interested in peace and measures to secure peace" than in finding ways to boost military appropriations. Although today's political establishment sanitizes those bribes by classifying them as legitimate contributions to campaigns or political action committees, the judgment is, if anything, truer now than when first rendered in the 1930s.

The Nye Committee characterized this cozy relationship between the military services, elected officials, and so-called merchants of death[14] as "an inevitable part of militarism."[15] More accurately, it represented a foretaste of the militarism that was to flower in the next century.

Since the Nye Committee issued its findings, things have only gotten worse. The sums involved have increased by several orders of magnitude as has Washington's eagerness to accommodate weapons makers with money to spread around. Popular disgust with the outcome and aftermath of World War I, along with fears of another war already on the horizon, had prompted Senator Gerald Nye to hold his hearings. Recent wars, affecting American warriors but not the American people, have produced no comparable climate and no political figure of real standing expressing Nye's moral outrage. A North Dakota populist, Nye denounced the munitions business as "an unadulterated, unblushing racket," one "none the less obnoxious" because government itself was in cahoots with racketeers.[16] He spoke harshly but truthfully. Today such a comment from a sitting senator has become almost unimaginable. In one way or another, they are all on the take.[17]

Deciphering the signals emanating from on high, military commanders responded accordingly. In war zones, moral and ethical considerations took a backseat to the more pragmatic concerns of getting on with the job. Largely oblivious to any implications for the military profession, the officer corps accommodated itself to ever-larger intrusions by crony corporations and profiteers into what had once been soldiers' business.

Colonel Theodore Westhusing was, however, an officer for whom accommodation did not come easily. After graduating third in the U.S. Military Academy class of 1983 and spending several years serving in the field army, Westhusing had attended graduate school at Emory University. There he earned a PhD in philosophy—the title of his dissertation was *The Competitive and Cooperative Aretai within the American Warfighting Ethos*—before returning to West Point as a professor in the Department of English and Philosophy.[18]

Westhusing's scholarship focused on the concept of military honor. Yet his preoccupation with this topic extended well beyond the academic. He invested soldierly honor with quasi-religious connotations. In an extended reflection published in 2003, Westhusing wrote that honor—consisting of "fidelity, the observation of promises, and truth-telling"—was "all-important for the warrior profession." To be sure, he recognized that "honor—like love—comes in both true and false forms." For the warrior, those false forms (mere loyalty to regiment, for example, or to some abstract Samurai code) could be "particularly bewitching." The genuinely honorable warrior rejected these false idols. "Sanctified through oaths," he manifested "benevolence." The true warrior, observed Westhusing, protected "the system of justice to which the citizens of his community owe their allegiance." Further, his concern toward his "comrades in arms is such that he will willingly lay down his life to protect them." Here the warrior's "actions achieve ultimate moral worth."[19]

In early 2005, Westhusing voluntarily left his academic post to serve a six-month tour of duty in Iraq. There, his conception of honor collided with a radically discordant reality. Westhusing found himself in a position akin to that of a priest assigned to a new parish who discovers in the church basement not scripture study classes but a brothel. Overnight, the good pastor finds himself in the prostitution business. Even more disconcerting, he soon learns that his bishop sees nothing amiss with the enterprise. The pews are full. Sunday collection returns remain robust. Why rock the boat?

From his office in Baghdad's "green zone," Westhusing's job was to oversee the training of Iraqi police officers. More specifically, he was to ensure that a company called USIS, contracted to conduct that training, was complying with the terms of its $79 million contract. USIS employees, all of them civilians, trained the police; "born to be a warrior," Westhusing policed the trainers.[20] It was not a relationship in which concerns about honor were likely to figure prominently.

Westhusing had a particular fondness for *The Killer Angels*, Michael Shaara's novel about the Battle of Gettysburg, and in particular for Shaara's portrayal of Robert E. Lee. For Westhusing, Lee was something of a *beau ideal*, the paladin of the warrior's code. Of

Lee's Army of Northern Virginia, Shaara had written, "In that camp, there is nothing more important than honor."[21] Fate had cruelly thrust Colonel Westhusing into a camp where honor qualified at best as an afterthought.

In May 2005, Westhusing received an anonymous letter, apparently from someone on the USIS payroll, alleging that the contractor was cheating the U.S. government and that its employees had engaged in serious human rights abuses. The charges enumerated in the letter were specific and detailed. Weapons and radios had gone missing. Staffing levels fell short of those promised and required. Trainers lacked necessary qualifications. More troubling still, while accompanying police patrols, USIS employees had murdered unarmed Iraqis in cold blood and then bragged about it. The company's sole aim, the anonymous writer said, was "to make as much money as they can [while] doing as little work as possible." As for Westhusing, the writer thought that he seemed pretty clueless: "not very bright," overly impressed with the former SEALs on the USIS payroll, and willing to "believe pretty much anything that they tell you."[22]

On May 28, Westhusing alerted his superiors, Lieutenant General David Petraeus and Major General Joseph Fil, to the charges contained in the letter. In doing so, he offered his own view of the matter. The allegations were unfounded, Westhusing believed. He had kept a close eye on things and felt certain that USIS was "complying with its contractual obligations." Of course, to acknowledge the other possibility—that USIS had engaged in willful and blatant wrongdoing—would be tantamount to admitting that he himself was either a dupe or personally complicit.[23]

Yet the anonymous allegations haunted Westhusing, who now seemingly felt tainted by his dealings with USIS. Honor had somehow been compromised. Normally even-tempered and agreeable, he became anxious and withdrawn. In meetings, he raged against "money-grubbing contractors" and angrily complained that "he had not come over to Iraq for this."[24] On June 5, 2005, after an especially contentious meeting with USIS representatives at Camp Dublin near Baghdad International Airport, Westhusing went to his trailer, put his service pistol to his head, and pulled the trigger. A USIS employee discovered him lying in a pool of blood, dead.

Investigators found an anguished suicide note addressed to Petraeus and Fil: "You are only interested in your career and provide no support to your staff," it charged. "I cannot support a [mission] that leads to corruption, human right abuses and liars. I am sullied—no more. I didn't volunteer to support corrupt, money-grubbing contractors, nor work for commanders only interested in themselves. I came to serve honorably and feel dishonored . . . I cannot live this way." Why serve, the note continued, "when you no longer believe in the cause, when your every effort and breath to succeed meets with lies, lack of support, and selfishness?" Beneath Westhusing's signature, the note concluded with a brief postscript: "Life needs trust. Trust is no more for me here in Iraq."

Army investigators confirmed that Westhusing had indeed committed suicide.[25] A separate inquiry by the army inspector general exonerated Petraeus and Fil of any transgressions.[26] USIS stayed in business. Case closed.

In essence, the army wrote off Westhusing's death as an inexplicable tragedy. Why would this upright officer take his life just a month before his tour of duty was scheduled to end? Why had he not just run out the clock, returning to West Point and a family he loved? No one could answer these questions. An army psychologist looking into the case concluded that Westhusing possessed a "surprisingly limited" ability to grasp the fact that for some Americans Iraq was a moneymaking venture, not an opportunity to demonstrate benevolence. Westhusing had clung to the belief "that doing the right thing because it was the right thing to do should be the sole motivator for businesses," at least when the business at hand was war.[27] The shrink knew better. In a war zone awash with profiteers, doing the right thing for the right reasons took a backseat to other more urgent and tangible imperatives.

Yet this cynical diagnosis mistook the symptoms for the disease. Grasping the significance of what was unfolding in Iraq actually did require a philosopher's perspective. Call it Westhusing's Theorem: *In a democracy, the health of the military professional ethic is inversely proportional to the presence of hired auxiliaries on the battlefield.* The pursuit of mammon and the values to which military professionals profess devotion are fundamentally incompatible and irreconcilable. Where profit-and-loss statements govern, devotion to duty, honor, and country inevitably takes a hit. Westhusing's encounter with this reality exposed the inadequacy of his own elaborately constructed idealism.

Westhusing's Theorem awaits definitive proof. Yet the experience of the Iraq War—unprecedented dependence on contractors coinciding with staggering malfeasance that the officer corps could not or would not control—qualifies at the very least as highly suggestive. For a true believer like Theodore Westhusing, becoming implicated in that malfeasance, even if indirectly, proved unendurable. In Iraq, he had discovered Westhusing's Theorem, and doing so cost him his life.

GETTING THE DIAGNOSIS RIGHT

The Iraq War has not added to the population of unknown soldiers memorialized at Arlington Cemetery. Yet if there will be no new unknown soldiers, there will be many forgotten ones. Put Colonel Westhusing—at the time of his death the senior-most casualty of the Iraq War—at the top of that list.

Now that the war in Iraq has ended (for the United States at least), Americans might ponder the question of what the loss of several thousand soldiers there signifies. I have grappled with that question myself, not altogether successfully. One imagines that it becomes more difficult still when a soldier dies not in battle but as a result of an accident or by his or her own hand. Such circumstances deprive the bereaved of the consolation, however negligible or contrived, of knowing that their loved one died a "warrior's death."

Theodore Westhusing did not die a warrior's death. Yet his death was a sacrificial act and should command the attention of anyone concerned about the health of the military profession. Here was the fire bell that rang in the night. Through his words and his own act of self-destruction, he warned of an impending cataclysm. Westhusing had not precisely followed Smedley Butler in becoming a "high class muscle-man for Big Business" or a "gangster for capitalism." Yet in Iraq he discovered that in forging its lucrative partnership with defense contractors, the army to which he had devoted his life had sullied itself. The stain was indelible. For Westhusing, this proved too much to bear.

For others, and especially for the topmost echelons of the officer corps, the bell rang to no avail. The army paused to mourn Westhusing's passing—in a handsome gesture, General Petraeus flew in from Iraq to attend the funeral service at West Point—but then just as quickly moved on. Westhusing became little more than "a buried footnote"—albeit a problematic one—appended to Petraeus's career, which continued on its upward trajectory.[28]

In 2010, Colonel Matthew Moten, a faculty colleague of Westhusing's at West Point who also happened to be serving in Iraq at the time of his friend's death (and who escorted his remains home), took a run at reviving Westhusing's cause. In an essay appearing in the journal *Foreign Affairs*, Moten decried the practice of allowing profit-motivated contractors to displace military professionals in performing functions traditionally reserved for soldiers. Conceding that the practice was now "so advanced within defense circles as to be almost beyond challenge," Moten nonetheless insisted that "it is wrong." Whether through ignorance or irresponsibility, the officer corps, he wrote, was opting for "short-term expediency over long-term professional health." The decision was one that soldiers would come to regret. "By contracting out many core functions," Moten warned, "the U.S. military is not only ceding its professional jurisdiction to private enterprise but . . . is also choosing slow professional death."[29]

Yet if Moten's case was well argued, his warning fell on deaf ears. Perhaps this was predictable. In many respects, the choices that really mattered had occurred long before the Iraq War. The real problem wasn't that Iraq had somehow allowed contractors to elbow soldiers aside and insinuate themselves onto the battlefield. Rather, it lay in a series of decisions, made decades earlier, committing the United States to a military system that proved incompatible with Washington's expectations of what U.S. military power ought to do. Cumulatively, these decisions, each in turn endorsed (or at least passively accepted) by citizens and soldiers alike, had placed the military profession in a bind from which it could not extricate itself.

As a consequence of Vietnam, the American people had jettisoned the tradition of the citizen-soldier. That was the first decision and arguably the most important. Accepting that decision as definitive, American military leaders devised and enthusiastically promoted the model of the warrior professional as the citizen-soldier's replacement. Then, in the wake of the Cold War, American political leaders—senior military officers concurring and the public generally happy to go along for the ride—embraced militarized globalism as the cornerstone of foreign policy. The United States was going to lead the world, with military power the principal means for enforcing its will. Only when the world proved less compliant than Washington expected and American warriors found themselves enmeshed in wars they proved unable to conclude did contractor encroachment on matters that soldiers had once claimed as their own become ruinous.

Westhusing, Moten, and other exponents of the military professional ethic correctly identified the threat posed by predatory contractors as existential in its implications. Yet vainly attempting to banish war profiteers from the battlefield will not provide a remedy. Rather, those concerned to avert further erosion of military professionalism face a clear-cut choice. The imperative is either to limit the nation's ambitions to those that a relatively small professional army can manage (which implies giving up on globalism) or to revive the citizen-soldier tradition (with globalism becoming contingent on a popular willingness to participate in war).

Military professionals have mistaken citizen-soldiers for their enemies. This tendency was especially pronounced after Vietnam. In fact, the citizen-soldier is the professional's truest ally. The enemy of the military ideal that Theodore Westhusing sought to preserve is unbridled ambition on Washington's part, expressing itself in an affinity for imperial adventurism that engenders massive corruption, while the American people sit idly by. Iraq was a case in point. Afghanistan is another. Reinstitute a military system that mandates shared sacrifice—people's war—and you'll have either fewer wars or the means to create a larger army. Either way, military professionals win.

Still, one wonders: How do those occupying the upper reaches of the national security apparatus and their profit-minded collaborators manage to get away with it? How do they succeed in perpetuating a "game" so manifestly rigged to suit their own purposes rather than contributing to the nation's well-being? A partial answer lies in the failings of the American intelligentsia.

10

TRAHISON DES CLERCS

Those who sit at the high table of American intellectual life pride themselves on their capacity to detect inconsistencies, contradictions, and hypocrisy. Yet that instinct does not encompass the nation's military system or the relationship between the military and society. There, complacency reigns. The prospect of a particular war may arouse attention, but Washington's penchant for war more generally largely escapes notice. So do the assumptions, ambitions, and arrangements—especially relating to the issue of who serves and sacrifices—which undergird that penchant.

One should take care not to overstate the role ideas play in the formulation of statecraft. Ideas as such—whether a strategy like "containment," a policy like "flexible response," or the vision of benign global hegemony to which neoconservatives swear fealty—rarely determine policy per se. Circumstances (however imperfectly understood) combined with expediency and a dollop of politics, partisan and bureaucratic, do. Yet ideas frame the environment in which statesmen interpret circumstances and justify their decisions. Out of the clash of theory and opinion, whether advanced by sober academics or inflammatory talk show hosts, come cues that policy makers consciously exploit or to which they subconsciously respond. Barack Obama did not invent the Obama Doctrine of counterterrorism any more than Bill Clinton invented the Clinton Doctrine of humanitarian intervention or George W. Bush the Bush Doctrine of preventive war. In each case, a president was merely adopting a concept that others had already devised, vetted, and promoted.

So it is no small thing that leading members of America's chattering classes find nothing objectionable in the way Washington parcels out responsibility for fighting the nation's wars. When it comes to military matters, what intellectuals care about is not how America raises its armed forces but when, where, and how to employ them.

In December 2002, for example, the journalist George Packer wrote a long essay for the *New York Times Magazine*, sampling opinion among liberal intellectuals—for Packer, a phrase synonymous with persons of enlightened sensibility—regarding the impending invasion of Iraq. Why among liberal thinkers he admired, Packer wondered, was there no deeply felt antiwar sentiment? None of the notables answering Packer's question—"the ones who have done the most thinking and writing about how American power can be turned to good ends as well as bad, who don't see human rights and democracy as idealistic delusions"— even mentioned U.S. military capacity or prowess as factors worthy of consideration. None paused to consider the possibility that the coercive propagation of liberal values abroad might undercut liberal values at home, especially given the fact that the chosen means of propagation was an army largely divorced from the American people. The bellicose Christopher Hitchens, more Trotskyist than liberal, declared that "Americanization is the most revolutionary force in the world" and expressed his enthusiasm for seeing

U.S. forces unleash that revolution in Iraq. Hitchens, Packer reported, had "plans to drink Champagne with comrades in Baghdad." Lacking comparable revolutionary zeal, Leon Wieseltier, longtime literary editor of the *New Republic*, was on the fence. He feared that Saddam Hussein's reputed weapons of mass destruction made war necessary, but worried about where armed intervention would ultimately lead. Yet the outcome was predetermined: "We will certainly win," he declared. For his part, Paul Berman, archfoe of radical Islam, shared none of Wieseltier's modest hesitation. The nation and the world were facing a new brand of totalitarianism. "The only possible way to oppose totalitarianism is with an alternative system, which is that of a liberal society," imposed if necessary at the point of a bayonet. Whether to trust George W. Bush's promises to democratize Iraq gave Berman pause; that some considerable number of American soldiers might get killed or maimed along the way did not.[1] Nor did the possibility that the existing American military system might prove ill suited to the task of foisting liberal values on illiberal nations. Berman contemplated the prospect of war with sublime confidence. As he commented elsewhere, invading Iraq offered the chance to "foment a liberal revolution in the Middle East." Doing a fair imitation of Secretary of State John Foster Dulles denouncing communist appeasers a half century earlier, Berman added that such a war could provide the means "to begin a roll-back of the several tendencies and political movements that add up to Muslim totalitarianism."[2]

Faced with war plans gone awry, the odd left-leaning hawk might later express doubts about that system, but even then only in passing. Richard Cohen offers a case in point. The *Washington Post* columnist supported the invasion of Iraq in 2003, then recanted when things went badly. By early 2011, Cohen—who decades earlier had served briefly as a reservist—was bemoaning the gap between the armed forces and society that enabled Washington to wage wars "about which the general public is largely indifferent." To maintain a military establishment that is "removed from society in general," he had concluded, offered a recipe for recklessness. "Had there been a draft, the war in Iraq might never have been fought—or would have produced the civil protests of the Vietnam War era. The Iraq debacle was made possible by a professional military and by going into debt. George W. Bush didn't need your body or, in the short run, your money."[3]

Yet not long after this epiphany, with civil war erupting in Syria, Cohen once again donned his liberal hawk's regalia, calling for "the United States to get involved in a muscular fashion." In 2011, with Iraq in mind, Cohen had written, "Little wars tend to metastasize." In 2012, with Iraq seemingly forgotten, he subscribed to another view, writing with assurance that if U.S. forces "hit Syria's command and control centers," they would trigger a "stampede" of defections by senior members of the hated regime of Bashar al-Assad. "Nothing so illuminates an exit sign as the certainty of defeat."[4] Back in 2011, Cohen worried that the United States had followed in the path of the Roman and British empires, "able to fight nonessential wars with a professional military in places like Iraq." In 2012, to fight another less than essential war that in Cohen's eyes had become an object of desire, the professional military was just the ticket.

In an earlier era, the GI army had been "of the people"—so at least liberals (prior to Vietnam) had pretended. For present-day liberals with itchy trigger fingers, "the troops" have become an abstraction, with the pretense of identifying with those who fight no longer necessary.

The point is not that the scribblings of Hitchens, Wieseltier, Berman, Cohen, and the like had any significant impact on decisions being made at the White House or in the Pentagon. Yet their assumptions regarding U.S. military power and their indifference to civil-military relationships reflected and served to reinforce attitudes in common circulation among elites of all stripes. Put bluntly, heavy-duty thinkers keen to put American power to work putting the world right can't be bothered to consider whether the nation's existing military system comports with the very values they are insistent upon propagating. By extension, their concern for the well-being of American soldiers ranks on a par with management's concern for the long-term health of NFL players. Brain injuries resulting from recurring concussion? It's not that no one cares. It's just that such considerations have taken a backseat to the imperatives of filling seats and boosting TV ratings. Similarly, in assessing the prospects of military action, militant liberals have in recent years accepted without serious question claims of U.S. martial omnipotence and shown little interest in considering what definition of *democratic* the current American approach to waging war can be said to satisfy. The overriding concerns of those eager to advance righteous causes lie elsewhere. Game on.

JOHN WAYNE AND JANE ADDAMS

A military composed of warrior-professionals suits the agenda of hawkish conservatives at least as well as hawkish liberals. For those who dream of liberating the oppressed abroad and reversing the corrupting tide of liberalism at home here is an instrument ideally suited to making those dreams come true. Not persuaded? Consider the views of the noted conservative commentator and *New York Times* columnist David Brooks.

Back in early 2003, eager to have the United States invade Iraq, Brooks mocked those expressing reservations or reluctance. "They want [George W. Bush] to show a little anguish," he wrote on the eve of war. "They want baggy eyes, evidence of sleepless nights, a few photo-ops, Kennedy-style, of the president staring gloomily through the Oval Office windows into the distance." As for Brooks, he wanted only action, and the sooner the better. "Bush gave Saddam time to disarm. Saddam did not. Hence, the issue of whether to disarm him forcibly is settled." [5] The journalist took for granted the ability of the United States military to settle matters forthwith.

Early signs of battlefield success affirmed such expectations. "One gets the impression," Brooks wrote just days after the invasion began, "that U.S. military dominance is now so overwhelming that the rules of conflict are being rewritten."[6] He derided the "ludicrous Vietnam comparisons [and] rampant quagmire forebodings" of namby-pambies not sharing his euphoria.[7] The president's decision to topple Saddam Hussein, Brooks felt certain, "represents what the United States is on earth to achieve. Thank God we have the political leaders and the military capabilities to realize the ideals that have always been embodied in our founding documents."[8]

On April 28, 2003, beating President Bush's "Mission Accomplished" speech by three days, Brooks declared that "the war in Iraq is over."[9] The political and cultural implications of victory promised to be profound. A collaboration between policy makers in Washington and troops on the battlefield had removed any last doubts as to American global dominion. Brooks sang the praises of "a ruling establishment that can conduct wars with incredible competence and skill." The United States, he enthused, was an "incredibly effective colossus that can drop bombs onto pinpoints, [and] destroy enemies that aren't even aware they are under attack."[10]

With Americans on the home front appropriately dazzled by what the troops had accomplished on the battlefield, Brooks's sensitive antenna detected a decisive shift in public sentiment. "One hears," he wrote, "of a growing distaste for the peace marchers . . .

driven by bile and self-righteousness [and] fundamentally out of step" with the rest of the country. To be in step was to support the troops, which necessitated supporting the war and the larger ambitions cultivated by the war's proponents. "Many college students seem to sense that these soldiers are accomplishing something for humanity, while all they are doing is preparing for business school."[11]

Implicitly acknowledging the distance separating young Americans who chose to serve in uniform from the young Americans choosing otherwise, Brooks made clear which group deserved his admiration. "Can anybody think of another time in history when a comparable group of young people was asked to be at once so brave, fierce and relentless, while also being so sympathetic, creative and forbearing?" Brooks couldn't, so he bestowed on the troops the secular equivalent of collective canonization. "They are John Wayne," he rhapsodized, "but also Jane Addams." Soldiers were paragons of virtue, their courage and altruism standing in stark contrast to the shallow, self-absorbed liberal culture that Brooks despised. "If anybody is wondering: Where are the young idealists? Where are the people willing to devote themselves to causes larger than themselves? They are in uniform in Iraq."[12] The gap between the military and society, in other words, was a good thing. It provided America with a great war-winning army and Americans with desperately needed exemplars of virtue.

Soon after Brooks published this paean to the American soldier, word of depraved and despicable acts at Abu Ghraib prison began to surface. Apparently, John Wayne and Jane Addams did not exhaust the range of possible role models to whom at least some American soldiers looked for inspiration. In an instant, the air went out of the liberation narrative that Brooks (and others) had been so earnestly plugging. Worse, contrary to his assurances, the war itself refused to end. Violent resistance to the American presence began to increase in both scope and intensity. Brooks's proclamation of victory turned out to be a case of premature journalistic ejaculation.

For a time, Brooks stubbornly stuck to his guns. "Come on, people," he urged in April 2004, "let's get a grip." Brooks disparaged the "Chicken Littles like [Democratic senators] Ted Kennedy and Robert Byrd [who] were ranting that Iraq is another Vietnam." He ridiculed the "pundits and sages [who] were spinning a whole series of mutually exclusive disaster scenarios: Civil war! A nationwide rebellion!" The American people needed to exhibit patience, allowing America's warriors to finish the job. "The task is unavoidable . . . The terrorists are enemies of civilization. They must be defeated."[13]

Yet as something approximating a civil-war-*cum*-national-rebellion ensued, Brooks changed his tune. "I never thought it would be this bad," he confessed less than a month after denouncing the Chicken Littles.[14] Reversing course, he concluded that the hawks had radically misunderstood the intended beneficiaries of America's ministrations. "While the Iraqis don't want us to fail, since our failure would mean their failure, many don't want to see us succeed either. They want to see us bleed, to get taken down a notch, to suffer for their chaos and suffering. A democratic Iraq is an abstraction they want for the future; the humiliation of America is a pleasure they can savor today."

Brooks now turned on the Bush administration, savaging it and the entire national security apparatus for gross incompetence. "A year ago, we were the dominant nation in a unipolar world. Today, we're a shellshocked hegemon." The fault lay with the people at the top. Errors of implementation had occurred in abundance. Even so, the cause remained a noble and necessary one. "We hawks were wrong about many things," Brooks grudgingly conceded. "But in opening up the possibility for a slow trudge toward democracy, we were still right about the big thing."[15]

In the difficult spring of 2004, Brooks clung to his slow trudge hypothesis. Whatever problems the United States was facing in Iraq, the imperative was to prevent any backsliding. "In this climate of self-doubt," Brooks worried, "the 'realists' of right and left are bound to re-emerge."

> They're going to dwell on the limits of our power. They'll advise us to learn to tolerate the existence of terrorist groups, since we don't really have the means to take them on. They're going to tell us to lower our sights, to accept autocratic stability, since democratic revolution is too messy and utopian.
>
> That's a recipe for disaster. It was U.S. inaction against Al Qaeda that got us into this mess in the first place. It was our tolerance of Arab autocracies that contributed to the madness in the Middle East.[16]

Just days later, however, Brooks threw in the towel. "We went into Iraq with what, in retrospect, seems like a childish fantasy," he announced.

> We were going to topple Saddam, establish democracy and hand the country back to grateful Iraqis. We expected to be universally admired when it was all over.
>
> We didn't understand the tragic irony that our power is also our weakness. As long as we seemed so mighty, others, even those we were aiming to assist, were bound to revolt. They would do so for their own self-respect. In taking out Saddam, we robbed the Iraqis of the honor of liberating themselves. . . .
>
> Now, looking ahead, we face another irony. To earn their own freedom, the Iraqis need a victory. And since it is too late for the Iraqis to have a victory over Saddam, it is imperative that they have a victory over us. If the future textbooks of a free Iraq get

written, the toppling of Saddam will be vaguely mentioned in one clause in one sentence. But the heroic Iraqi resistance against the American occupation will be lavishly described, page after page. For us to succeed in Iraq, we have to lose.[17]

Here again, the pronoun demands attention: Who exactly was this *we* to which Brooks insistently referred? In practical terms, his *we* did not include the American people. It was not *us*. It was instead the U.S. military. Brooks had previously depicted that military as unbeatable; now, bizarrely, he wanted it to accept defeat in order to boost Iraqi self-esteem. Having insisted that military success in Iraq was essential to preserve Iraqis from a terrible fate, he now proposed that U.S. troops embrace failure in order to provide Iraqis with a heroic narrative in which they could take pride. Victory once had been a certainty; now it had become undesirable.

In short order, he went a step farther: the United States, it turned out, had not known how to win in the first place. "Let's face it," he wrote in May 2004, "we don't know whether all people really do want to live in freedom." Humility was now the order of the day. "We don't know whether Iraqis have any notion of what democratic citizenship really means. We don't know whether they hear words like freedom, liberty and pluralism as deadly insults to the way of life they hold dear. We don't know who our enemies are."[18]

With 150,000 American troops attempting to put out the fires touched off by the U.S. invasion, "the destiny of Iraq is largely out of our hands," Brooks concluded. "The U.S. tried to hand a new Iraq back to the Iraqis. We failed."[19] By early 2005, Brooks was edging precariously close to the realist camp that he had denounced less than a year before.

Sprinkling his columns with references to "irony" as he channeled the spirit of Reinhold Niebuhr, Brooks might have chosen to reflect deeply on all that had gone wrong in Iraq and in his own calculations. Was the main problem simply incompetence on the part of George W. Bush, his advisers, and his generals—a splendid initiative squandered through faulty implementation? Or did failure derive from deeper causes, perhaps a fundamental misunderstanding of war or history or human nature itself? Or could the problem lie, at least in part, with a perversely undemocratic military system that condemned soldiers to waging something like perpetual war at the behest of a small coterie of Washington insiders, while citizens passively observed from a safe distance?

Sharing the inclination of his countrymen, Brooks chose not to engage in any searching inquiry at all. Rather than reflecting on Iraq, he looked for new fields in which to test his theory of using military power to spread American ideals while redeeming American culture at home. Afghanistan—a war already under way for more than a decade—presented just the second chance he was looking for. Based on a quick visit, Brooks concluded that Afghanistan was nothing like Iraq. U.S. military efforts there promised to yield a different and far more favorable outcome. "In the first place," he wrote during his government-arranged reporting trip in early 2009, "the Afghan people want what we want . . . That makes relations between Afghans and foreigners relatively straightforward. Most [U.S.] military leaders here prefer working with the Afghans to the Iraqis. The Afghans are warm and welcoming." Even better, they actually "root for American success."

That wasn't all. In contrast to its fumbling performance in Iraq, the U.S. military had now fully mastered the business of winning hearts and minds. Know-how had displaced ineptitude, with the union of John Wayne and Jane Addams now fully consummated. Further, with the distraction of Iraq now out of the way, the troops in Afghanistan possessed the wherewithal needed for "reforming the police, improving the courts, training local civil servants and building prisons." As Brooks put it, "we've got our priorities right."

Furthermore, "the Afghans have embraced the democratic process with enthusiasm." Unlike the recalcitrant and ungrateful Iraqis, they were teachable and amenable. Brooks commended President Obama for "doubling down on the very principles that some dismiss as neocon fantasy: the idea that this nation has the capacity to use military and civilian power to promote democracy, nurture civil society and rebuild failed states." Granted, the trial run in Iraq had gone badly, but why cry over spilled milk? Besides, Iraq had served as an education of sorts. Brooks felt certain that trying again in Afghanistan would yield a better outcome. In short, that war was "winnable."[20]

Yet Afghanistan proved no more winnable than Iraq had been, at least not within the limits of what the United States could afford and the American public was willing to pay. The U.S. troops who burned Korans, defiled Taliban corpses, and gunned down innocent civilians in shooting sprees made it difficult for Afghans to appreciate the Jane Addams side of the American soldier. As for John Wayne, Hollywood had thought better than to film him urinating on dead enemy fighters. By 2012, an epidemic of "green-on-blue" incidents—Afghan security forces murdering their U.S. counterparts—revealed the absurdity of Brooks's blithe assertion that Afghans "want what we want" and "root for American success."[21] What most Americans wanted was to be done with Afghanistan.[22] In hopes of arranging a graceful withdrawal, they might allow Washington to prolong the war a bit longer, but with the usual terms fixed firmly in place: only so long as someone else's kid does the fighting and future generations get stuck with the bill.

ENABLERS

None of this implies that American writers and public intellectuals succumbed en masse to militarism. On the contrary, ever since the Cold War ended, a cadre of thoughtful observers had warned against the "superpower temptation" of inordinate ambition, while expressing skepticism regarding Washington's growing penchant for using armed force.[23] Even larger numbers spoke out against specific government actions, Bush's decision to invade Iraq in 2003 offering a notable example.

However imperfectly, the course of events over the past decade has largely vindicated the views of these critics. Whatever your opinion of Patrick Buchanan's politics, in warning against the folly of turning the Global War on Terrorism into a grand crusade against evil, the anti-interventionist conservative turned out to be more right than wrong.[24] The same might be said of Buchanan's left-wing counterparts such as Boston University's Howard Zinn and Yale's Immanuel Wallerstein. Already in mid-2002, Zinn was predicting that attacking Iraq, a country with "no logical connection" to the events of 9/11, would serve chiefly to "further inflame anger against the United States" throughout the Islamic world.[25] At about the same time, declaring that the "Pax Americana is over," Wallerstein correctly forecast that an invasion of Iraq would find Washington biting off considerably more than it could chew.[26]

Yet apart from allowing them to say "I told you so," the critique they fashioned barely dented the reigning foreign policy consensus. There are several reasons for this. First, Washington did not take well to the charge that in mortgaging America's well-being to U.S. military prowess it had committed a fatal error. After all, the mortgage papers had long since been signed, and the terms suited Washington just fine. Second, many ordinary citizens bridled at the suggestion that Iraqi and Afghan beneficiaries of "liberation" might with justification see U.S. forces as unwelcome intruders, with Washington's claims of high-mindedness no more credible than similar claims made by previous waves of foreign invaders. Allow for the possibility that American purposes do not differ greatly from those of the British, French, or Germans in the heyday of European colonialism, and the moral basis for exercising "global leadership" begins to look shaky.

But there exists a third reason as well: efforts by intellectuals (or quasi intellectuals) eager to do the bidding of power more than offset the efforts of those intent on holding power accountable. Writing in 1917, soon after the United States had entered World War I, the essayist Randolph Bourne identified the issue with devastating precision. For a particular category of intellectuals, entranced by the aphrodisiac of power, independence is a pose willingly abandoned when the prospect of "relevance" beckons. Faced with an opportunity to "matter," they rush to conform. For a considerable number of American intellectuals, 9/11 offered just such an opportunity.

Bourne bitterly opposed U.S. involvement in World War I. A great majority of American intellectuals had shared that position—until President Woodrow Wilson declared it incumbent upon the United States to join hands with Great Britain, France, and Russia in making "the world safe for democracy." With that, the intellectual stampede in favor of war commenced.

Wilson depicted the war as a contest pitting civilization against barbarism. Not buying this line, Bourne took out after intellectuals who did. "Only in a world where irony was dead," he wrote, "could an intellectual class enter war at the head of such illiberal cohorts in the avowed cause of world-liberalism and world-democracy." In his view, the issues at stake had little to do with liberal democratic values. To believe otherwise was to allow a faux patriotism to eclipse independent judgment. Yet once Congress declared war, a demand for slavish compliance swept through editorial offices and faculty lounges like a hurricane. "In a time of faith," Bourne wryly observed, "skepticism is the most intolerable of all insults."

Here was testing time for members of the American intelligentsia. In Bourne's eyes, they flunked. Allowing the passions of the moment to displace reasoned analysis, they became enablers. During the years of U.S. neutrality, he continued,

> our intellectual class might have ... spent the time in endeavoring to clear the public mind of the cant of war, to get rid of old mystical notions that clog our thinking. We might have used the time ... for setting our house in spiritual order, [turning] not to the problem of jockeying the nation into war, but to the problem of using our vast neutral power to attain democratic ends ... without the use of the malevolent technique of war. They might have failed. The point is that they scarcely tried.

Abandoning principle in order to serve power, intellectuals instead devised arguments to justify "what is actually going on or what is to happen inevitably tomorrow," all in the vague hope that as "responsible thinkers" they might be of some use to the mighty, while "those who obstructed the coming of war" were "cast into outer darkness." The demands of power were severe and uncompromising: "Be with us, ... or be negligible [and] irrelevant."[27]

This describes the dilemma facing American intellectuals before and after 9/11. Not all succumbed to the allure of putative relevance, of course. Some opted for integrity over influence. But others did succumb, and through their rabble-rousing books, columns in the prestige press, and appearances as knowing TV commentators, they helped make respectable Washington's infatuation with armed force as *the* preferred tool of statecraft.[28] By extension, they suppressed any inclination to probe the large political and moral defects of the nation's military system, content merely to add their voices to others in professing admiration for "the troops." For this group, jockeying the nation into war became a priority, if not an obsession. Even today, they cling to that priority despite successive disappointments and despite the travails the troops have endured, in which, needless to say, they themselves have not partaken. Although this might not meet the strict definition of treason, it certainly qualifies as grotesque and contemptible irresponsibility.

11

DRONING ON

Since the creation of the all-volunteer military, America's warriors have not lacked for opportunities to practice their craft. In the eyes of the policy elite, an elite military combines the best features of both thoroughbred and draft horse. It's optimized to run fast and work hard. As a result, over the past forty years, decision makers in Washington have launched U.S. forces into a bewildering array of contingencies. Let's do a quick inventory.

Since the draft ended, along with Iraq (twice) and Afghanistan, U.S. ground forces have intervened for stays ranging from weeks to years in Lebanon, Grenada, Panama, Somalia, Haiti, Bosnia, and Kosovo. Smaller groups on special missions secretly entered Iran in 1980 (a humiliating failure) and Pakistan in 2011 (a celebrated success). Other long-duration, quasi-covert operations occurred in El Salvador, Honduras, and Colombia. In 2012, with little fanfare, President Obama added to the list of South of the Border interventions, sending U.S. Marines to patrol the western coast of Guatemala as part of the "war on drugs."[1] In addition to many of the places listed above, American bombs and missiles have on various occasions in recent decades rained down on Libya, the Sudan, and Yemen. The American military narrative becomes so crowded that some episodes just get lost in the shuffle. Who today remembers the 1975 *Mayaguez* incident, in which eighteen Americans were killed while attempting to regain control of a container ship shanghaied by the Khmer Rouge? Or how about the "Tanker War" of 1984–88? Highlights included a crippling Iraqi attack on the USS *Stark*—with Washington readily accepting Saddam Hussein's apology for killing thirty-seven American sailors— and the USS *Vincennes* shooting down an Iranian commercial airliner—with Washington refusing to apologize for killing 290 passengers and crew.

Tuned-out Americans are generally no more familiar with these events, their causes, or their connection to one another than they are with why the First Seminole War happened or how it led to the Second Seminole War. Mainstream commentary on foreign policy provides little by way of remedial instruction. Once Washington identified Saddam Hussein as a villain in 1990, U.S. support for Iraq during its war of aggression against Iran in the 1980s—that's why President Ronald Reagan so generously accepted Saddam's mea culpa in the *Stark* affair—retained no more relevance than U.S. connivance with the freebooters who overthrew Hawaii's Queen Liliuo-kalani in 1893. Once George W. Bush promulgated (and Barack Obama subsequently endorsed) the depiction of present-day Iran as a country led by madmen, the possibility that the Iranians might have some legitimate gripes with the United States—the downing of Iran Air flight 655 in 1988 along with the CIA's overthrow of a democratically elected government in 1953 offering two glaring examples—became inadmissible.

Taken together, just what "story" does this bloody sequence of wars, skirmishes, and kerfuffles tell? Upon examination, three distinct threads emerge, the first relating to *ideology*, the second to *geography*, the third to *operational purpose* (and by extension methods). To trace these narrative threads is to appreciate just how far in the wrong direction the military exertions of the past four decades have carried the United States.

IDEOLOGY: THE RISE OF BOYKINISM

From the late 1940s to the late 1980s, communism provided the overarching ideological rationale for American globalism and for the deployment of U.S. military power. With the passing of the Cold War and the demise of the Soviet empire, that rationale vanished. In the 1990s, the national security elite sought to define threats in nonideological terms, with rogue states, ethnic strife, and mere instability among the concepts floated. None of these provided a sufficiently robust justification for continued American globalism.

With the advent of the Global War on Terrorism, however, ideology came roaring back. Islamism succeeded communism as the body of beliefs that, if left unchecked, threatened to sweep across the globe with dire consequences for freedom. So at least members of the national security establishment professed to believe. Yet as a rallying cry, Islamism presented real difficulties. As much as policy makers struggled to prevent Islamism from merging with Islam in the popular mind, some Americans—whether genuinely fearful or mischief-minded—saw this as a distinction without a difference. Efforts by the Bush administration to work around this problem by framing the post-9/11 threat as *terrorism* ultimately failed because the term offered no explanation for motive. And motive seemed somehow bound up with matters of religion.

During the Cold War, religion had figured as a prominent component of American ideology. Communist antipathy toward religion helped invest both anticommunism and the Cold War foreign policy consensus with their remarkable robustness. That communists were godless sufficed to place them beyond the pale. For many Americans, the Cold War derived its moral clarity from the conviction that here was a contest pitting the God-fearing against the God-denying. Since we were on God's side, it appeared axiomatic that God should repay the compliment.

From time to time during the decades when anticommunism provided much of the animating spirit that informed policy, American strategists (culturally Judeo-Christian, although not necessarily believers themselves), drawing on the theologically correct proposition that Christians, Jews, and Muslims all worship the same God, sought to enlist Muslims in the cause of opposing the godless. The Soviet invasion of Afghanistan in 1979 seemingly presented an ideal opportunity to do just that. To inflict pain on the Soviet occupiers, Washington threw its weight behind the Afghan resistance, religious zealots that U.S. officials styled as "freedom fighters." When the Red Army eventually withdrew in defeat, God's verdict seemed plain to all. The God-fearing had prevailed. Yet not long after the Soviets pulled out, Afghan freedom fighters morphed into the fiercely anti-Western Taliban, providing sanctuary to Al Qaeda, formerly part of the anti-Soviet phalanx, but now claiming to act at God's behest as it plotted attacks on the United States.[2] Previously an asset to the formulation of foreign policy, religion suddenly threatened to become a net liability.

So where to situate God in the post-9/11 ideological frame posed challenges for U.S. policy makers, not least of all George W. Bush, who believed, no doubt sincerely, that God had chosen him to save America in its time of maximum danger. Unlike communists, Islamists did not deny God's existence. Far from it: they embraced God with startling fervor. Indeed, in their vitriolic denunciations of the satanic United States and in perpetrating acts of anti-American violence, radical Islamists audaciously presented themselves as God's avenging agents. In confronting the Great Satan, they claimed to be serving God's purposes.

This debate over who actually represented God's will was one that the administrations of George W. Bush and Barack Obama studiously sought to avoid. Engagement in such a debate would implicitly suggest that a religious war was under way. Instead, U.S. officials resolutely and repeatedly insisted that the United States was not at war with Islam per se. Still, Washington's repeated denials notwithstanding, among some considerable number of Muslims the suspicion persisted.

Not without reason: appearing with some frequency, inflammatory events—in 2010, the hullaballoo over the "Ground Zero Mosque" in lower Manhattan; in 2011, the promotion of "International Burn a Koran Day" by the pastor of a Gainesville-based Christian church; in 2012, the circulation of an American-produced video slandering the Prophet Muhammad—reinforced such suspicions. However earnestly U.S. officials dismissed such controversies as the work of a few fanatics, reality proved more complicated—and more troubling.

Consider the case of Lieutenant General William G. "Jerry" Boykin, an eleventh-century Christian crusader reborn as a twenty-first-century American warrior.

While still on active duty in 2002, this highly decorated army officer spoke in uniform at a series of some thirty church gatherings during which he offered his own take on President Bush's famous rhetorical question "Why do they hate us?" General Boykin's perspective differed markedly from the position taken by his commander in chief: "The answer to that is because we're a Christian nation. We are hated because we are a nation of believers." On another such occasion, the general recalled an encounter with a Somali warlord who claimed to enjoy Allah's protection. The warlord was deluding himself, Boykin told his coreligionists, and was sure to get his comeuppance. "I knew that my God was bigger than his. I knew that my God was a real God and his was an idol." As a Christian nation, the general insisted, the United States would succeed in overcoming its adversaries only if "we come against them in the name of Jesus."[3] As far as Boykin was concerned, the war on terrorism was indeed a religious war; to pretend otherwise was foolhardy.

When Boykin's remarks caught the attention of the press, denunciations rained down from on high, as the White House, the State Department, and the Pentagon hastened to disassociate themselves from the general's statements. Yet subsequent indicators suggested that, however crudely, Boykin was expressing views shared by more than a few of his fellow citizens.

One such indicator came immediately: despite the furor, the general kept his very important Pentagon job as deputy undersecretary of defense for intelligence, suggesting that the Bush administration considered his transgression minor. While he may have spoken out of turn, for a senior U.S. military officer to demean Islam did not evidently rise to the level of fireable offense.[4]

A second indicator came in the wake of Boykin's eventual retirement from active duty. In 2012, the influential Family Research Council (FRC) in Washington hired him to serve as its executive vice president. Devoted to "advancing faith, family, and freedom," the council professes an emphatically Christian outlook. The FRC is not a fringe organization. It falls well within the conservative mainstream, much as, say, the American Civil Liberties Union falls within the left-liberal mainstream. Its events routinely attract Republican Party heavyweights. In Washington circles, it wields real clout.

Those who brought Boykin on board as the FRC's chief operating officer obviously found nothing offensive in the former general's pronounced views on Islam. In all likelihood, by hiring him, the council meant to send a signal: on matters where its new COO claimed expertise—above all, on how to prosecute the war on terrorism—the FRC was not going to pull any punches. Imagine the NAACP electing Nation of Islam leader Louis Farrakhan as its national president, and you get the idea. Spit-in-your-eye political incorrectness had become a virtue.

In a broader sense, the organization's embrace of General Boykin makes it impossible to write off manifestations of Islamophobia as tomfoolery perpetrated by a maniacal fringe. As with the supporters of Senator Joseph McCarthy during the early days of the Cold War, those who express hostility toward Islam, whether through words or actions, dare to convey openly attitudes that others in far greater numbers quietly nurture. To put it another way, what Americans in the 1950s knew as McCarthyism has reappeared as what we might call Boykinism, with the FRC as its main institutional base.

Historians differ passionately over whether McCarthyism represented a perversion of anticommunism or its truest expression. Similarly, present-day observers may disagree as to whether Boykinism represents a somewhat fervent or utterly demented response to the Islamist threat. Yet this much is inarguable: just as the junior senator from Wisconsin in his heyday embodied a nontrivial strain of American politics so, too, does the former special ops warrior turned "ordained minister with a passion for spreading the Gospel of Jesus Christ."[5]

Notably, as Boykinism's leading exponent, the former general espouses views that bear a striking resemblance to those favored by the late senator. Like McCarthy, Boykin believes that while enemies beyond America's gates pose great dangers, the enemy within poses a still greater threat. "I've studied Marxist insurgency," he declared in a 2010 video. "It was part of my training. And the things I know that have been done in every Marxist insurgency are being done in America today." Comparing the United States as governed by Barack Obama to Stalin's Soviet Union, Mao Zedong's China, and Fidel Castro's Cuba, Boykin charged that under the guise of health-care reform the Obama administration was secretly organizing a "constabulary force that will control the population in America." Designed to be larger than the United States military, it was to function just as Hitler's brownshirts had in Germany.[6] This vast totalitarian conspiracy was, of course, unfolding while innocent and unsuspecting Americans slumbered.

The evidence Boykin offered to support his charge was on a par with the evidence Senator McCarthy offered to support his claim to "have here in my hand a list of two hundred and five people . . . known to the Secretary of State as being members of the Communist Party." That is to say, no proof at all. Yet as in the 1950s, the absence of hard evidence only served to confirm the conspiracy's nefarious existence.

In Joe McCarthy's day, how many Americans endorsed his conspiratorial view of world and national politics? It's difficult to know for sure, but enough in Wisconsin to secure his reelection in 1952, by a comfortable majority of 54 to 46 percent. More important, enough to strike fear into the hearts of politicians who quaked at the thought of McCarthy fingering them for being "soft on communism."

How many Americans endorse Boykin's comparably inflammatory views of both Islam and American politics? Again, it's difficult to tell, but enough to persuade the FRC's funders and supporters to hire him, confident that doing so would burnish rather than tarnish the organization's brand. Certainly, adding Boykin's name to the list of officers did not damage its convening power. The council's 2012 "Values Voter Summit," held just weeks after he took the council's reins, featured luminaries such as Republican vice presidential nominee Paul Ryan, former Republican senator Rick

Santorum, House Majority Leader Eric Cantor, and Representative Michele Bachmann—along with Jerry Boykin himself, who opined on "Israel, Iran, and the Future of Western Civilization."[7] When Republican presidential candidate Mitt Romney huddled with a group of prominent "social conservatives," the delegation included Boykin.[8]

Did their appearance at the FRC's podium signify that these Republican heavyweights subscribed to Boykinism's essential tenets? Did his tête-à-tête with Boykin mean that Romney himself was an Islamophobe? Not any more than those who exploited the McCarthyite moment to their own political advantage—Richard Nixon, for example—necessarily agreed with all of the senator's reckless accusations. Yet the presence of leading Republicans on an FRC program alongside the general and Romney's willingness to consult him certainly suggested that they found nothing especially objectionable in his worldview, that he was, in fact, their kind of guy.

Where comparisons between McCarthyism and Boykinism break down is in assessing their impact. McCarthyism wreaked havoc mostly on the home front, instigating witch hunts, destroying careers, and trampling on civil liberties, while imparting to American politics even more of a circus atmosphere than usual. In terms of foreign policy, the effect of McCarthyism, if anything, was only to cement an already established anticommunist consensus. The senator's antics didn't create enemies abroad; McCarthyism merely affirmed that communists were indeed the enemy, while jacking up the political price of daring to think otherwise.

Boykinism, in contrast, makes its impact felt abroad, rather than at home. Unlike McCarthyism, it doesn't strike fear in the hearts of incumbents seeking reelection. Attracting General Boykin's endorsement or provoking his ire hasn't determined the outcome of any election and is unlikely to do so. Yet in its various manifestations Boykinism provides some of the kindling that sustains anti-American sentiment in the Islamic world.

Doggedly sticking to their script, American presidents and secretaries of state may praise Islam as a religion of peace and even tout past U.S. military actions ostensibly undertaken on behalf of Muslims. Yet with their credibility among Arabs, Iranians, Afghans, Pakistanis, and others in the Islamic world about nil, these officials are wasting their breath. The Boykinism that some Americans profess confirms what many Muslims are already primed to believe, namely, that American values and Islamic values are irreconcilable. Certainly, that describes General Boykin's own view, one with which, according to polling data, nearly half of all Americans concur.[9]

When it comes to providing an ideological justification for U.S. policy, in other words, the pivot from communism to Islamism that occurred between 1989 and 2001 has yielded at best problematic results. No longer a source of internal solidarity as during the Cold War, religion has become an impediment, notably complicating any action involving the use of U.S. military power.

Recall that during the Cold War, ideology—rough agreement on the meaning of freedom, including religious freedom—had made it possible to create such useful fictions as the West and the Free World. Among inhabitants of these culturally heterogeneous realms, religion had become a private matter, not a hot-button political issue. It was, therefore, irrelevant to the question of whether Western Europeans, Japanese, and South Koreans were willing to permit U.S. military garrisons in their midst. Since the end of the Cold War, by contrast, the presence of U.S. forces among the peoples of the Islamic world has served chiefly as a reminder of religion-centered ideological dissonance—sharp disagreement over what freedom should permit and religious duty entail. In simplest terms, many Muslims resent occupation by armed infidels.

Resolving that disagreement—and by extension repairing America's negative image in the Islamic world—poses monumental challenges. An obvious first step might be to stop engaging in behavior that Muslims find offensive, like stationing infidels in their midst. Yet for members of a national security elite committed to the proposition that positioning American troops on foreign soil solves problems, acknowledging that such deployments may actually exacerbate them requires stores of honesty and self-awareness they do not possess. It's like asking a boxing fan to acknowledge that the "sweet science" is no science at all but an artifact of primordial savagery.

The substantial numbers of vocal Americans who do not themselves buy the ideological argument deployed to justify U.S. intervention in the Islamic world—that our conception of freedom (including religious freedom) is ultimately compatible with theirs—encourage Muslims to reach precisely the same conclusion. In that regard, the supporters of Jerry Boykin and the supporters of Osama bin Laden are of a like mind. Together, they ensure that further reliance on armed force as the favorite tool in the toolbox of U.S. policy will only compound the errors that contributed to 9/11 itself and have marred the post-9/11 era.

GEOGRAPHY: INVENTING THE GREATER MIDDLE EAST

During the first half of the twentieth century, the United States twice intervened in ongoing European wars, dispatching its citizen-soldiers to prevent Germany from dominating that continent. Today, with war in Europe all but unimaginable, the United States acquiesces in a defanged Germany moving inexorably toward a first-among-equals position within the European Union.

During the second half of the twentieth century, the United States twice sent its citizen-soldiers to fight in East Asia, first to prevent a communist takeover of South Korea and subsequently to prevent a communist takeover of South Vietnam. Neither of these wars proved popular. So beginning in the 1970s, the United States opted to accommodate rather than oppose the major East Asian communist power, the People's Republic of China. At least for a time, this proved very popular indeed with many American entrepreneurs and most American consumers.

Beginning in 1980, however, Washington's decades-long preoccupation with Europe and East Asia began to give way. With the promulgation of the Carter Doctrine in January of that year, the Persian Gulf took its place alongside the Fulda Gap and the Korean Demilitarized Zone as a place that mattered. Imperceptibly at first, but then with increasing speed over the course of the next decade, the U.S. strategic center of gravity shifted away from the twin poles of Western Europe and East Asia and toward the Greater Middle East (GME).

Religion and culture rather than traditional geopolitics determine the GME's boundaries. The region is nothing if not expansive. Extending from western Africa to the southern Philippines, it stretches across eleven time zones and encompasses several dozen countries, each containing a Muslim majority or a large (and invariably restive) Muslim minority.

The region derived its original strategic significance from the presence of valuable resources (primarily but not exclusively oil) and the crucial transit routes (sea-lanes and pipelines) necessary to transport those resources once extracted. Although competition among great and middle-sized powers first drew in the United States, well before 9/11 Washington had found new grounds for considering the GME important. Resources remained a key consideration, but so did the perception that the region had become an incubator of radicalism and a source of instability. Violence joined oil as the GME's principal export.

In response, beginning with the Carter administration, the United States embarked on a series of experiments, hoping to devise ways of suppressing violent radicalism while fostering pro-Western stability. The implications of these experiments for the U.S. military have been almost entirely unhappy.

For Americans in uniform, the Greater Middle East now became the primary zone of conflict, both active and prospective. Between 1945 and 1980, U.S. forces suffered virtually no casualties in the GME due to hostile action. During the 1980s, that changed. Since 1990, U.S. forces have suffered virtually no casualties *outside* that region.

For bureaucracies, of course, shifting priorities are a godsend, offering opportunities to expand. The Pentagon welcomed the discovery—or invention—of the Greater Middle East, rife with potential for justifying the creation of new programs, offices, weaponry, and commands. The armed forces wasted little time in seizing those opportunities.

Until the 1980s, in the pecking order of Pentagon regional headquarters, U.S. European Command (EUCOM) had ranked first, with U.S. Pacific Command (PACOM) not far behind. As senior American proconsul in Europe, the four-star EUCOM commander general wore a second hat. He was NATO's Supreme Allied Commander Europe (SACEUR), as splendid a title as the military world has ever conferred.

In those days, the Pentagon had not even bothered to create a command for the Greater Middle East. The SACEUR attended to the region in his spare moments. Today, to manage its sundry activities in the Islamic world, the Pentagon maintains two regional headquarters: U.S. Central Command (CENTCOM) and U.S. Africa Command (AFRICOM).

Back at his headquarters in Belgium, a U.S. officer still carries the title SACEUR, but he no longer reigns supreme over anything. Indeed, during the past three decades, the U.S. forces at his disposal have shrunk by 80 percent. Many of those that remain rotate back and forth between training bases in Germany or Italy and theaters like Afghanistan where the real action occurs, the SACEUR functioning less as their commander than their landlord.[10] As the SACEUR keeps up appearances while presiding over his dwindling domain, the commanders of CENTCOM and AFRICOM increasingly exercise the sort of authority that once was SACEUR's. Although he may still live in a fancy house, no one much cares what the SACEUR has to say. England's queen and Japan's emperor might empathize.

That the Pentagon should divvy up the Greater Middle East, delineating the jurisdiction of adjacent proconsulates, was entirely consistent with standard U.S. military practice. Ever since World War II, the Pentagon has made a habit of overlaying a U.S. military map on the world's political map. Subdividing the globe into right-sized compartments facilitated the effective projection of U.S. might—so at least the national security establishment came to believe. In Washington, this belief achieved canonical status, no more subject to question than the Catholic doctrine of papal infallibility or the Baptist belief in scriptural inerrancy. The emergence of CENTCOM and AFRICOM as important regional commands testified to the persistence of this conviction.

Created in 1983, U.S. Central Command today presides over an "area of responsibility" encompassing twenty nations, as it seeks to "provide a stronger, more lasting solution in the region." With this goal in mind, CENTCOM—according to its mission statement—"promotes cooperation among nations, responds to crises, and deters or defeats state and nonstate aggression, and supports development and, when necessary, reconstruction in order to establish the conditions for regional security, stability, and prosperity."[11]

Progress toward achieving these ambitious goals remains elusive. General James Mattis, CENTCOM commander in 2012, opened his annual "Posture Statement" with this admission: "Change is the only constant and surprise continues to be the dominant force in [a] region [plagued by] poor governance, a large youth demographic bulge and insufficient economic opportunity, and the social construct between governments and their people breaking down in numerous places." Making matters worse, Mattis conceded that "the lack of a sustainable solution to the Palestinian-Israeli conflict is a preeminent flame that keeps the pot boiling in the Middle East." Expressing regret that 612 U.S. troops had been killed under his command, along with another 8,251 wounded, he consoled himself with the thought that combat was producing "a generation of elite leaders," without, however, venturing to say what exactly such sacrifices had accomplished. Still, the general had no doubt that "persistent military engagement" would enable CENTCOM "to protect vital interests, prevent future conflict, ensure access in the event of a crisis and invest in future regional security." The key to success lay in trying harder, sending more U.S. troops on more missions to more places. For General Mattis, light eternally glimmered at the end of CENT-COM's tunnel.

AFRICOM, created in 2007 and encompassing fifty-four countries, emphasizes a similar can-do spirit. According to a "Failed States Index" cited by General Carter Ham, in his 2012 commander's "Posture Statement," Africa is home to fourteen of the world's twenty weakest states. Governments across the continent "lack the capacity or political will to effectively address demographic, political, social, and economic challenges, including population growth, rapid urbanization, persistent internal conflicts, widening income inequality, burgeoning political demands, widespread disease, and increasing demands for essential resources." But General Ham, like

General Mattis, professed optimism. "Through sustained engagement," AFRICOM was going "to create a security environment that
promotes stability, improved governance, and continued development."[12]

From the general's lips to God's ears, one might respond. In the
face of such grandiose statements, a cynic might suggest that
engagement is a euphemism, properly translated as "preparing for
war"—extended reconnaissance operations during which U.S.
forces familiarize themselves with trouble spots that may someday
become the site of shoot-to-kill "contingency operations." A cynic
might also note that when engagement produces results other than
those promised, the Pentagon's reflexive response is not to rethink
the enterprise but to subdivide the world further. Thus do new
commands proliferate, providing employment for more generals
and admirals managing more engagement programs, while back
home the Pentagon creates offices to provide oversight and support. Small wonder that "the Pentagon" has long since outgrown
the Pentagon.

In the years ahead, unless the Greater Middle East suddenly
becomes a garden of peace and goodwill, we can no doubt look
forward to AFRICOM dividing into northern (mostly Muslim)
and southern (mostly not) components, with CENTCOM splitting
into a Near East Command (centered on the Persian Gulf) and a
Southwest Asia Command (centered on the Durand Line separating Afghanistan and Pakistan). What we cannot look forward to is
anyone questioning the sense of the basic endeavor. In its quest to
control an unruly world, the Pentagon—acting in the name of the
American people—slices and dices that world into smaller and
smaller segments, while neglecting to assess the actual costs and
benefits of the persistent meddling that it terms engagement. In
this way, the regionalization of U.S. military policy serves to perpetuate sterile thinking.

OPERATIONAL PURPOSE: MIMICKING ISRAEL

Peace means different things to different governments and different countries. To some it suggests harmony based on tolerance and mutual respect. To others it serves as a euphemism for *dominance*, quiescence defining the relationship between the strong and the supine.

In the absence of actually existing peace, a nation's reigning definition of peace shapes its proclivity to use force. A government committed to peace-as-harmony will tend to employ force only as a last resort. The United States once subscribed to this view—or beyond the confines of the Western Hemisphere at least pretended to do so.

A nation seeking peace-as-dominion will use force more freely. This has long been an Israeli predilection. Since the end of the Cold War and especially since 9/11, it has become America's as well. As a consequence, U.S. national security policy increasingly conforms to patterns of behavior pioneered by the Jewish state. In employing armed force, decision makers in Washington (regardless of party) claim the sort of prerogatives long exercised by decision makers in Jerusalem (regardless of party). Although this "Israelification" of U.S. policy may have proven beneficial for Israel, it has not been good for the United States, nor will it be.

Credit Israeli statesmen with this much: they express openly views that American statesmen hide behind clouds of obfuscation. Here, for example, is Israeli Prime Minister Benjamin Netanyahu in June 2009 describing what he called his "vision of peace": "If we get a guarantee of demilitarization . . . we are ready to agree to a real peace agreement, a demilitarized Palestinian state side by side with the Jewish state."[13] Now, the inhabitants of Gaza and the West Bank, if armed and sufficiently angry, can annoy Israel, though not destroy it or even do it serious harm. By any measure, the Israel Defense Forces (IDF) wield vastly greater power than the Palestinians could possibly muster. Still, from Netanyahu's perspective, "real peace" becomes possible only if Palestinians guarantee that their putative state will forgo even the most meager military capabilities. Your side disarms, our side stays armed to the teeth; that in a nutshell describes the Israeli prime minister's conception of peace.

Netanyahu asks a lot of Palestinians. Yet however baldly stated, his demands reflect long-standing Israeli thinking. For Israel, peace derives from security, which must be absolute and assured. *Security* thus defined requires not military advantage but military supremacy.

Given the importance that Israel attributes to security, anything that threatens it requires anticipatory action, the earlier the better. The IDF attack on Iraq's Osirak nuclear reactor in 1981 provides one example. Israel's destruction of a putative Syrian nuclear facility in 2007 provides a second; its 2013 attack on a Syrian convoy allegedly delivering weapons to Hezbollah offers a third.

Yet alongside perceived threat, perceived opportunity can provide sufficient motive for anticipatory action. In 1956 and again in 1967, Israel attacked Egypt not because its leader, the blustering Colonel Gamal Abdel Nasser, possessed the capability (even if he proclaimed the intention) of destroying the hated Zionists, but because preventive war seemingly promised a big Israeli payoff. In the first instance, the Israelis came away empty-handed; their British and French allies caved in the face of pressure imposed by an angry President Dwight D. Eisenhower, and Israel had no choice but to follow suit. In 1967, Israelis hit the jackpot operationally, albeit with problematic strategic consequences. Subjugating a substantial and fast-growing Palestinian population that Israel could neither assimilate nor eliminate imposed heavy burdens on the victors.

Adherence to this knee-to-the-groin paradigm has won Israel few friends in the region and few admirers around the world (Americans notably excepted). The likelihood of this approach eliminating or even diminishing Arab or Iranian hostility toward Israel appears less than promising. That said, the approach has thus far succeeded in preserving (and even expanding) the Jewish state: more than sixty years after its founding, Israel persists and even prospers. By this rough but not inconsequential measure, the Israeli security concept, nasty as it may be, has succeeded.

What's hard to figure out is why the United States would choose to follow Israel's path. A partial explanation may lie with the right-ward tilt of American politics that began in the late 1970s, affecting the way both Republicans and Democrats have approached national security ever since. Among hawks in both parties, Israel's kick-ass pugnacity struck a chord. As a political posture, it can also win votes, as it did so memorably for Ronald Reagan, campaigning for the presidency back in 1980, in the midst of the Iran hostage crisis. As a presidential candidate, Reagan not only promised unstinting support for Israel but also projected a "take no guff" attitude that came right out of that country's political playbook. The contrast with Jimmy Carter, who was seemingly taking a lot of guff from abroad, could hardly have seemed starker. That Reagan proceeded to trounce Carter was a lesson not lost on candidates in subsequent elections.

Over the course of the Bush/Clinton/Bush/Obama quarter century, following in Israel's path describes precisely what Washington has done. A quest for global military dominance, pursued in the name of peace, and a proclivity for preemption, justified as essential to self-defense, pretty much sums up America's present-day MO.

Israel is a small country with a small population and no shortage of hostile neighbors. The United States is a huge country with an enormous population and no enemy within several thousand miles of its borders (unless you count the Cuban-Venezuelan Axis of Ailing Autocrats). Americans have choices that Israelis do not. Yet in disregarding those choices, the United States stumbled willy-nilly into an Israel-style condition of perpetual war—with peace increasingly tied to unrealistic expectations that adversaries and would-be adversaries will comply with Washington's demands for submission.

Israelification got its kick-start with George H. W. Bush's Operation Desert Storm, that triumphal Hundred Hour War likened at the time to Israel's triumphal Six Day War. As we have noted, that victory fostered illusions of the United States exercising perpetually and on a global scale military primacy comparable to what Israel has enjoyed regionally. Soon thereafter, the Pentagon announced that it would settle for nothing less than what it termed *full spectrum dominance*.

Bill Clinton's contribution to the process was to normalize the use of force. During the several decades of the Cold War, the United States had resorted to overt armed intervention only occasionally. Although difficult today to recall, back then whole years might pass without U.S. troops being sent into harm's way. During Clinton's two terms in office, however, intervention became commonplace.

The average Israeli had long since become inured to reports of IDF incursions into southern Lebanon or Gaza. Now the average American became accustomed to reports of U.S. troops battling Somali warlords, supervising regime change in Haiti, or occupying the Balkans. Yet the real military signature of the Clinton years came in the form of air strikes. Employing bombs and missiles to blast targets in Afghanistan, Bosnia, Serbia, and Sudan, but above all Iraq, became the functional equivalent of Israel's reliance on airpower to punish "terrorists" while avoiding the risks and complications of putting troops on the ground.

In the wake of 9/11, George W. Bush, along with Secretary of Defense Rumsfeld, a true believer in full spectrum dominance, set out to liberate or—take your pick—pacify the Islamic world. The United States followed Israel in assigning itself the prerogative of waging preventive war. Although depicting Saddam Hussein as an existential threat, the Bush administration also viewed Iraq as an opportunity. By destroying his regime and occupying his country, the United States would signal to other recalcitrants the fate awaiting them should they mess with or defy Uncle Sam.

More subtly, in going after Saddam, Bush was tacitly embracing a long-standing Israeli conception of deterrence. For the United States during the Cold War, deterrence had meant conveying a credible threat (the prospect of nuclear retaliation) to dissuade your opponent (the Soviet Union) from hostile action. Israel had never subscribed to that view. Influencing the behavior of potential adversaries required more than signaling what Israel *might* do if sufficiently aggravated or aggrieved; influence was exerted through punitive action, ideally delivered on a disproportionate scale. Hit the other guy first, if possible. Failing that, whack him several times harder than he hit you; not the biblical injunction of an eye for an eye, but both eyes, an ear, and several teeth, with a kick in the groin thrown in for good measure.[14] The aim of these "retribution operations" was to send a message: screw with us and this will happen to you. This message Bush intended to convey when he ordered the invasion of Iraq in 2003.

Unfortunately, Operation Iraqi Freedom, launched with all the confidence that had informed Operation Peace for Galilee, Israel's equally ill-advised 1982 incursion into Lebanon, landed the United States in an equivalent fix. Or perhaps a different comparison applies: the U.S. occupation of Iraq triggered violent resistance similar to that which the IDF faced as a consequence of its occupation of the West Bank. Two successive intifadas gave the Israeli army fits. The insurgency in Iraq (along with its Afghan sibling) gave the American army fits, too.

Neither the Israeli nor the American reputation for martial invincibility survived these encounters. What did survive was Washington's belief, imported from Israel, in the efficacy of anticipatory action. The United States now subscribed to the view that the key to successful self-defense was to attack the other guy first. The dictum that force should be a last resort might still apply to others, but after 9/11 it no longer applied to the United States. Nothing that actually occurred in Iraq, the first large-scale application of the Bush Doctrine of preventive war, altered that conviction.

While he was in office, George W. Bush adamantly rejected the arguments of those who characterized the intervention in Iraq as a mistake or a failure. Senator Barack Obama had forthrightly labeled the war a mistake of the first order, a position that became the foundation for his run for the presidency in 2008. Yet when the war became his, President Obama proved less inclined to criticize its conduct. By the time it finally ended in 2011, Obama was spinning the mission in Iraq as anything but a flop or a fiasco. Speaking at Fort Bragg, North Carolina, he described the war as "one of the most extraordinary chapters in the history of the American military," culminating in "an extraordinary achievement, nearly nine years in the making," to wit, the emergence of "a sovereign, stable and self-reliant Iraq."[15]

At best half-truths tailored to suit Obama's soldier audience, his claims nonetheless meshed with the inclinations of Americans unwilling to face a painful truth: that the culmination of the Iraq War had yielded a verdict almost identical to that of Vietnam. As in Vietnam, U.S. forces had not succumbed to outright defeat. Yet whatever solace Americans might take from that fact paled in comparison with the massive policy failure the United States had again suffered.

Characterizing the Iraq War as a success, however tenuous or qualified, undoubtedly made that disaster easier to swallow, while also shielding the Bush Doctrine of preventive war from critical scrutiny. On that score, Obama expressed no regret and apparently harbored no second thoughts. Bush's successor was not about to forfeit the option of striking first. In that regard, the Gates Doctrine—no more land invasions in the Middle East or Asia—may have amended but did not revoke the Bush Doctrine. Gates had no wish to limit U.S. freedom of action in employing force. He merely pointed to the need to devise different techniques for doing so. Like Israel, when it comes to "anticipatory defense," the United States shows no signs of relinquishing its self-proclaimed entitlement.

The Israelification of U.S. policy also extended to the means employed in waging war. As its own preferred approach to preventive action, Israel had for decades relied on a powerful combination of tanks and fighter-bombers. In more recent times, however, it has sheathed its swift sword in favor of the knife between the ribs. Why deploy lumbering armored columns when a missile launched from a single Apache attack helicopter or a bomb fixed to an Iranian nuclear scientist's car can do the job more cheaply and with less risk? Thus has targeted assassination eclipsed conventional military methods as the hallmark of the Israeli way of war.

Here too, lagging behind by a couple of decades, the United States has conformed to Israeli practice. By the time Barack Obama succeeded Bush in 2009, most Americans (like most Israelis) had lost their appetite for invading and occupying countries. Yet as a political rallying cry, "Never Again Iraq" no more foreshadowed a dovish turn in U.S. policy than had "No More Vietnams."

Nobel Peace laureate or not, Obama had no intention of forfeiting the expanded latitude to use force bequeathed to him by his predecessor. Yet to maintain his freedom of action—affirming that war was the commander in chief's business, with others invited to butt out—Obama needed to avoid the mistakes that had tripped up Bush. By reducing the likelihood of costly quagmires, the Israeli approach again offered an attractive model.

With this in mind, Obama demonstrated a keen preference for small-scale operations rather than big wars, quick strikes rather than protracted campaigns, actions conducted in secret rather than under the glare of publicity. The *Washington Post* columnist Michael Gerson got it right. "Obama wants to be known for winding down long wars," he observed. "But he has shown no hesitance when it comes to shorter, Israel-style operations. He is a special ops hawk, a drone militarist."[16]

With his affinity for missile-firing drones, the president established targeted assassination as the very centerpiece of U.S. national security policy. With his predilection for commandos, he expanded the size and mandate of U.S. Special Operations Command, which under Obama maintained an active presence in some 120 countries.[17]

That Obama should further the Israelification of U.S. policy was not without irony. After all, personal relations between the president and his Israeli counterpart, Prime Minister Netanyahu, were famously chilly. Yet in Yemen, Somalia, the frontier regions of Pakistan, and other far-flung places, Obama showed that when it came to using force, he and Netanyahu occupied the same page. Both were committed to the proposition that if you keep whacking bad guys long enough, a positive outcome should eventually ensue.

In the meantime, for the president, the downside of targeted assassination appeared minimal. True, from time to time an errant U.S. missile might kill the wrong people (to include children) or American commandos might "take out" some bystanders along with Mr. Big. Yet back home, reported incidents of this type elicited a muted response. As far as the American media were concerned, the death of a few nameless Somalis or Pakistanis carried about as much newsworthiness as a minor traffic accident. As a determinant of presidential standing, a U.S. fighter-bomber inadvertently wiping out an Afghan wedding party lagged far behind a slight uptick in the unemployment rate.

The government of Israel (along with ardently pro-Israeli Americans like Michael Gerson) may view the convergence of U.S. and Israeli national security practices with some satisfaction. Washington's now-prevailing definition of *self-defense*—a self-assigned mandate to target anyone anywhere thought to endanger U.S. security—is exceedingly elastic. As such, it provides a certain cover for equivalent Israeli inclinations. And to the extent that the American roster of enemies overlaps with Israel's—Iran providing an obvious example—the hope always remains that military action ordered by Washington just might shorten Jerusalem's "to do" list.

Yet where does this all lead? "We don't have enough drones," writes the columnist David Ignatius, "to kill all the enemies we will make if we turn the world into a free-fire zone."[18] And if Delta Force, the Green Berets, Army Rangers, Navy SEALs, and the like constitute, in the words of one SEAL, "the dark matter . . . the force that orders the universe but can't be seen," we probably don't have enough of them either.[19] Unfortunately, the Obama administration has seemed willing to test both propositions.

EYELESS IN GAZA

Accept at face value the narrative described by any of these several threads, and U.S. military policy over the past several decades acquires a certain logic. Those needing further assurance that the various and sundry dots do indeed connect can consult piles of official statements issued by the White House, the State Department, and the Pentagon, the content of which can be summarized in a single sentence: trust us; we know what we are doing. Think tankers and pundits respond to such claims with clarifications, modifications, or mild dissents, but the overall impact of their critique is to affirm, rather than overturn, official views. On Friday afternoons and Sunday mornings, at high-toned journalistic venues, panels and roundtables comb through the events of the past seven days and do likewise. The weekly bits of wisdom offered by Shields and Brooks or Brooks and Dionne—"So *should* the United States attack Iran? You first, E. J."—serve ultimately to endorse Washington's prevailing worldview.

Embrace that worldview and you'll find no reason to doubt that America, acting at God's behest, is still out there doing God's work, no matter what some disgruntled foreigners might say. You'll take it for granted that proliferating international crises should rightly entail the further proliferation of overseas military activities. You won't need to ask how preventive war, long condemned as immoral, became almost overnight morally permissible. And you won't find it odd that assassination, once considered beyond the pale, has now emerged as a core function of the chief executive, the president himself choosing individual targets and periodically updating the nation's "kill list."[20]

Yet superficial logic cannot conceal an absence of overall direction and purposefulness. Reject Washington's self-aggrandizing worldview, and the fundamental irrationality of its policies becomes unmistakable. The fact is that the three threads don't connect, and worse yet they don't lead anywhere except to ever more arduous efforts undertaken at ever escalating costs. Since the end of the Cold War, even with people in Washington busily moving the tiller back and forth, the American ship of state has been adrift and foundering, with the sacrifices of U.S. troops serving mostly to increase the rate at which the ship is taking on water.

The contrast with Vietnam is instructive. There, successive presidents erred by grotesquely misapplying a fundamentally sound strategy. Shortly after World War II, containing Soviet power had emerged as the lodestar of U.S. policy. Measured in those terms, Vietnam qualified as a stupefying blunder—the wrong war, in the wrong place, against the wrong enemy. Yet despite the inappropriate application of containment to a civil war in postcolonial Indochina, the overall strategy devised by Harry Truman (who inaugurated the U.S. commitment to Vietnam) retained its utility up to and beyond the era of Gerald Ford (who presided over the liquidation of that commitment). For decades, containment endowed U.S. policy with at least a modicum of coherence.

With the passing of the Cold War, the last vestiges of coherence vanished. Granted, considered in isolation, efforts by U.S. troops to rescue the downtrodden, overthrow dictators, or fight terrorists possessed a cursory plausibility. After all, back in 1992, Somalis really *were* starving. Slobodan Milošević and Saddam Hussein really *were* bona fide bad guys. Prior to 9/11, the Taliban *had* provided sanctuary to Al Qaeda. Yet taken together, these episodes, along with all the other military misadventures of recent decades, do not even remotely amount to a strategy worthy of the name. When it comes to basic policy, there may be threads, but there is no fabric.

Reflecting on the mind-set in 1960s Washington that gave rise to Vietnam, the literary critic Alfred Kazin once wrote, "Power beyond reason created a lasting irrationality."[21] Kazin's observation applies in spades to the period following the Cold War. With the collapse of communism, Washington convinced itself that the United States possessed power such as the world had never seen. Democrats and Republicans alike professed their eagerness to

exploit that power to the fullest. A sustained bout of strategic irrationality ensued, magnified and reinforced by the events of 9/11.
Sadly, the principal achievement of President Obama, who came
to office promising something better, has been to perpetuate that
irrationality.

12

AMERICAN CHARACTERS

Toward the beginning of his book *After Virtue,* the philosopher Alasdair MacIntyre introduces the concept of *characters* and reflects on their importance. "*Characters,*" he writes, "are the masks worn by moral philosophies." They describe "those social roles which provide a culture with its moral definition." Characters by no means command universal assent. Yet those who celebrate and those who despise a particular character "unwittingly collaborate as a chorus in the theatre of the present." Through characters, "moral and metaphysical ideas and theories assume . . . an embodied existence in the social world."[1]

Writing in 1981, MacIntyre identified the reigning characters in Western, and especially American, culture as the Rich Aesthete, the Manager, and the Therapist. In the United States, the passage of time has diminished the centrality of all three. A new trio has emerged in their stead: the Celebrity, the Geek, and the Warrior. These figures provide contemporary American society with at least a simulacrum of moral definition. Of the three, the warrior has the lowest profile but may well exercise the greatest importance, imputing a sense of purposefulness to an increasingly disordered society.

Who doesn't love celebrities? After all, they provide vicarious escape from an everyday existence that social critics and ad agency copywriters join hands in depicting as confining and banal. As an antidote to anomie, nothing beats glamour. If not endowing life with meaning, glamour at least infuses it with sizzle. Celebrities exude and define glamour, no matter how fleeting and ephemeral. The most important social function of celebrities is simply to appear, presenting themselves to be discovered, admired, adored, gossiped about, criticized, ridiculed, and ultimately pitied (often in precisely that sequence). They satisfy our itch for fantasy and our appetite for schadenfreude. We worship them when they are on their way up and follow them no less avidly when they crash and burn—when Britney Spears, head shaven, beats a car with a baseball bat; a bleary-eyed Lindsay Lohan gets hauled into court for the umpteenth time; or Katie leaves Tom standing high and dry. And we love them (yet again) if they manage to drag themselves out of the mire to appear "clean and sober" on the red carpet or gorgeously arrayed, if carefully airbrushed, on the cover of *Vogue*. And for those who can't manage full recovery, there's always reality TV to offer a not-to-be-sniffed-at consolation prize.

Hollywood remains today, as it has been for decades, celebrity central. Yet celebrity has moved well beyond the world of entertainment. Celebrity-athletes who reprise the time-honored rise-and-fall narrative (O. J. Simpson, Tiger Woods, Lance Armstrong) rivet our attention. Rock-star politicians (Bill and Hill dominate the category) enjoy an exalted status, eliciting the same over-the-top response as rock-star musicians. Then there are the instances of cross-pollination, the merger between actress and NBA star or supermodel and NFL quarterback, elevating the celebrity quotient of both parties and feeding an even greater craving to peer into their lives. In Boston, where I teach, the leading daily newspaper routinely informs its readers (typically with accompanying photograph) when Gisele Bündchen walks her son through the Common or Tom Brady goes bike riding along the Charles River. In the city I call home, the doings of the Bündchen-Brady household qualify as newsworthy indeed.

If the celebrity offers momentary escape from the quotidian, the geek promises empowerment. As used here, *geek* refers to the moguls of the information age who have demonstrated a genius for converting bytes into dollars: Steve Jobs, Bill Gates, Mark Zuckerberg, Jeff Bezos, and their imitators. Yet it also applies to the far more numerous and largely anonymous meme queens who through blogs, forums, social networking sites, instant messaging, and video streaming drive a culture that is moored to nothing more than irreverent whimsy and jeering ridicule. The appeal of this culture lies in its very impermanence. What's not new is by definition passé.

The geek has largely succeeded in convincing Americans, especially the young and the hip, that instantaneous access to information holds the key to personal fulfillment. In practice, the promised empowerment all too frequently translates into subservience and subordination, a compulsion to tend to the beeps, buzzes, and vibrations of objects supposedly designed to do our bidding. Whether the thickening of the electronic web that envelops us serves to increase the accumulated storehouse of wisdom remains unproven, to put it mildly, the social media fad offering a case in point.

In contrast to the celebrity or the geek, the profile of the warrior does include a prominent moral component. The warrior is the one *character* actually connoting character, providing assurance that America has not lost its ability to produce brave, self-sacrificing idealists.

Yet in performing that function, the warrior has become something other than a mere soldier. Indeed, the warrior has eclipsed the soldier.

To appreciate the distinction, consider two instances, separated by more than a half century, when *Time* magazine selected the American fighting man/person as its Man/Person of the Year. The first occurred during the early stages of the Korean War. When *Time* designated "G. I. Joe as Man of the Year" for 1950, developments on the battlefield were actually looking grim. Communist China had intervened, and U.S. forces were careening southward in disarray.[2] The second occasion occurred during the early stages of the Iraq War. *Time*'s collective designation of U.S. troops as Person of the Year for 2003 came at a moment when that conflict, too, had taken a turn for the worse. U.S. forces were struggling to suppress a growing insurgency. The difference in *Time*'s coverage speaks volumes about the evolving image and status of the Americans sent to fight our wars.

In its first-of-the-year issue for 1951, *Time* described U.S. forces in Korea as "the nearest approach to a professional army that the U. S. had ever sent into war." Yet the content of *Time*'s cover story belied that statement, depicting troops who were at once dutiful but doubtful, willing but less than enthusiastic, not terribly competent but capable in extremis of rising to the occasion. "The U. S. fighting man" sent to Korea, observed *Time*, "was not civilization's crusader, but destiny's draftee." Having no particular desire to fight, he viewed the war itself as "a terrifying affront." The GI was a bundle of contradictions: "soft and tough, resourceful and unskilled, unbelievably brave and unbelievably timid, thoroughly disciplined and scornful of discipline." *Time* freely acknowledged the GI's shortcomings. "His defects were many, serious—and understandable." Not least among them was an inadequate level of training, for which commanders compensated through a lavish reliance on matériel. As "the most comfort-loving creature who had ever walked the earth," the American soldier "went forth into battle, brandishing his chocolate bars [and] his beer cans."[3]

Still, *Time* concluded, "he had proved himself able to endure the thrusts of a brave and well-led enemy."[4] Illustrating the article and bearing persuasive witness to that judgment were sixteen small black-and-white photos, each hardly larger than a postage stamp. Battlefield portraits taken by famous *Time-Life* photographers like David Douglas Duncan and Carl Mydans, most showed drawn and haggard foot soldiers who had seemingly found little glory in war. By no means masters of all they surveyed, they could at least claim to have survived.

Time's first-of-year issue for 2004 took a decidedly different tack. To judge from the images in its pages, a reader in 1951 might conclude that the army in Korea consisted entirely of white males. A half century later, the magazine proudly designated U.S. forces "the most diverse military in our history," depicting U.S. forces in Iraq as a harmonious blend of black, brown, and white, male and female. Better still, they were "all volunteers, in contrast to most nations."[5]

Gone were the grainy black-and-white snapshots. Florid, large-format images showed neatly groomed, well-turned-out, and remarkably well-fed young people, both on the job and off-duty. On operations, they carried (or were encased in) high-tech gear that emphasized their technological sophistication. No one appeared haggard, hungry, or in need of a shower.

In one photograph, an armed American searches an Iraqi family's "sleeping quarters for guns or suspicious stores of cash" while the "residents watch warily." In another, an army captain "listens as an Iraqi woman begs for the release of her son, who has been taken into custody." In a palace once belonging to Uday Hussein, Saddam's son, a battalion commander and his staff peer at overhead images of Baghdad as they "plan a move against insurgents." Together, observed *Time*, these troops "are the face of America, its might and goodwill, in a region unused to democracy."[6]

Declaring the Iraq War "an expression of American idealism in all its arrogant generosity," *Time* depicted those troops as the agents of that idealism and generosity, without any of the arrogance. "They are the bright sharp instrument of a blunt policy." Not too blunt, however, *Time* assuring its readers that "the campaign of shock and awe was always aimed at mind and heart."[7]

An essay by the distinguished military historian John Keegan provided the cherry atop *Time*'s coverage. Although carrying the title "The Making of the American G. I.," the piece actually described the GI's demise, explaining how the citizen-soldier had given way to the warrior-professional, a development that Keegan heartily endorsed. "There is something Kiplingesque about the modern American warrior," he began. "He is a volunteer and a professional, as the long-serving regular of Rudyard Kipling's day was." In that regard, he was an apt successor to "Kipling's archetypal soldier, Tommy Atkins." Like Tommy, the American warrior feels a "personal relationship with his Commander in Chief," he wrote, thereby equating George W. Bush with Queen Victoria. "Above all, like Tommy, he ships out. Ordered to a strange corner of the world, often at the ends of the earth, he packs his kit, says his farewells and departs. He does not ask how long he will be away or where he is going or why. If the President gives the word, that is enough."

These new warrior-professionals differed fundamentally from the citizen-soldiers who had fought in World War II, Korea, or Vietnam. "America's armed forces are becoming imperial," Keegan continued, adding reassuringly that this was occurring "without their country's becoming imperialist." Barely containing his enthusiasm, he concluded on an implicitly imperial note. "Pax

Americana, like Pax Britannica," he wrote, "is guaranteed by a body of servicemen and -women who have no equal elsewhere on the globe."[8] Here was a fighting force suited for safeguarding, and perhaps Americanizing, the world.

In Keegan's considered assessment, the troops fighting in Iraq at the beginning of the twenty-first century had far more in common with British soldiers upholding Victoria's nineteenth-century empire than they did with the GIs in Korea at the midpoint of the twentieth century. In 1951, *Time* had gone out of its way to specify that Americans in uniform were *not* civilization's crusaders; by 2004, they had evidently become just that, even if for reasons of political correctness the magazine had banished from its pages any actual reference to crusades.

In fact, Keegan's essay ought to have given American readers pause. After all, the army that enforced the British Pax had achieved a rather mixed record of success, losing decisively to an armed rabble at places like Saratoga, Yorktown, and New Orleans and subsequently enduring disasters on widely scattered battlefields from Afghanistan and the Crimea to Sudan and the Transvaal. Why having present-day American warriors replicate this experience should qualify as a good idea might seem self-evident to a Briton like John Keegan. Yet any of *Time*'s American subscribers with even a modest knowledge of British imperial history might well have entertained doubts. Kipling himself knew what Keegan was choosing to overlook: keeping in line (even while purporting to uplift) the peoples Tommy Atkins disparaged as wogs is an ugly, thankless, demeaning, and ultimately futile task.[9]

REPEALING THE THREE NO'S

"America is not to be Rome or Britain," insisted the historian Charles Beard in 1939. "It is to be America."[10] Seven decades on,

Beard's sentiment has a quaint ring to it. Americans have become accustomed to their country asserting "global leadership"— shorthand for doing what Rome and Britain once did—with the heavy lifting consigned to a small but obliging warrior class.

Indeed, without the warrior, the entire enterprise collapses. Absent the warrior who fights without asking "where he is going or why," assertions of global leadership become unsustainable. Absent the myth of that warrior's indomitability, evidence that recent wars have depleted America's power while undercutting its prosperity becomes irrefutably obvious. Absent the insistence that among warriors virtue remains alive and well, the moral confusion pervading society—to which neither celebrity nor geek offers an antidote—becomes impossible to ignore.

American warriors may not win wars, but they do perform the invaluable service of providing their countrymen with an excuse to avoid introspection. They make second thoughts unnecessary. In this way, the bravery of the warrior underwrites collective civic cowardice, while fostering a slack, insipid patriotism. In the words of a hit country song, Americans

> salute the ones who died, and the ones that gave their lives,
> so we don't have to sacrifice all the things we love . . .
> like our chicken fried, cold beer on a Friday night,
> a pair of jeans that fit just right and the radio up.[11]

Just as in World War II, fried food and pop music still figure as homely surrogates for American freedom. Back then, however, Americans accepted fighting for freedom as their job; today, with freedom still their birthright, they expect someone else to do the fighting.

This division of labor is no longer working, if it ever did. Sold on the basis of economy, the professional military has turned out to be a bad bargain, fiscally but also politically and morally. As a character, the warrior has proven a costly disappointment. Americans may choose to pretend otherwise, but wishful thinking won't change the facts.

Encouraging such wishful thinking will be the institutions that benefit from existing arrangements: the national security state, the military-industrial-congressional complex, and the mushrooming private security sector. Apart from the odd military officer stricken in retirement with Smedley's syndrome, the people who wield influence within these institutions have no incentive for seeing anything amiss.

Is the past prologue? If so, here is what Americans can look forward to: more needless wars or shadow conflicts sold by a militarized and irresponsible political elite; more wars mismanaged by an intellectually sclerotic and unimaginative senior officer corps; more wars that exact huge penalties without yielding promised outcomes, with the consequences quickly swept under the rug even as flags flutter, fighter jets swoop overhead, the band plays the "Marines' Hymn," and commercials tout the generosity of beer companies doing good works for "the troops."

Averting this dismal fate will not be easy. But here's one place to begin: repeal the three no's that have defined the American military system since the advent of the all-volunteer force. In place of the three no's, substitute three affirmative commitments.

Instead of *we will not change*, Americans should revert to a concept of citizenship in which privileges entail responsibilities. Among those responsibilities, one in particular stands out: an obligation to contribute to the nation's defense when the country is at risk or when interests said to be essential to the American way of life require the use of military power.

Instead of *we will not pay*, Americans should fund their wars on a pay-as-you-go basis. Payment can take several forms. Citizens can pay higher taxes, forgo benefits, or reduce consumption. The rule of thumb should be this: any war not worth paying for is not worth fighting.

Instead of *we will not bleed*, Americans should insist upon fielding a citizen army drawn from all segments of society. The creation of the all-volunteer force reduced the importance of securing a popular buy-in as a prerequisite for military action. In Washington, this latitude fed an appetite for armed intervention. Curbing that appetite will require the restoration of popular leverage in matters relating to war. There is but one way to do this: abandon the model of the warrior-professional with his doppelgänger the private security contractor. General McChrystal's belated discovery is correct. When it comes to war, citizens *should* have skin in the game. Only then can they expect to have any say in how (and whether) the game gets played.

How exactly might recruitment for a citizen army work? One approach is through conscription, with *all* able-bodied young men and women eligible for service but only *some* actually selected. Imagine a lottery with Natasha and Malia Obama at age eighteen having the same chance of being drafted as the manicurist's son or the Walmart clerk's daughter.

A less heavy-handed, broader, and more inclusive approach would be through a program of national service in which *all* able-bodied eighteen-year-olds participate, with *some* opting for the military and the rest choosing other service opportunities: preserving the environment, caring for the sick and elderly, assisting the poor and destitute, or joining the Peace Corps. Some could groom our national cemeteries. Others might work as aides in VA hospitals or staff facilities that provide shelter to homeless vets. Some national service personnel might carry assault rifles; others would empty bedpans or pass out bed linens.

Whether relying on conscription or national service to raise such a force, a two-year military term of enlistment would provide ample time to acquire and employ most soldierly skills. Crewing a tank or an artillery piece, conducting patrols or ambushes are not rocket science. Certain specialties—flying an airplane is one obvious example—require longer periods of training. Becoming a pilot, therefore, would entail a more extended period of service, undertaken voluntarily. Yet the majority of the rank and file would consist of those serving two-year terms, with a follow-on cohort taking their place as they return to civilian life.

Critics will complain that relying on a citizen army will make it difficult to sustain protracted campaigns in far-off places like Iraq and Afghanistan. Just so. It will be incumbent upon civilian and military leaders to make the case to citizen-soldiers (and their parents) for long, drawn-out, inconclusive wars in far-off places. No doubt this will pose a challenge.

Yet the mere attempt to formulate such an explanation could well open up a larger conversation about what it means to "be America" in the twenty-first century. Those committed to the proposition that the United States has succeeded Rome and Britain understandably favor warrior-professionals for imperial expeditions, conducted, of course, under less incendiary labels. The United States really has no choice in the matter, they will insist. Has not Providence itself singled out this country to play a dominant role in world affairs?

Viable alternatives to the current all-volunteer system simply do not exist, they will claim, and are inconceivable in twenty-first-century America. On this point, they will have good reason to be adamant. Change the military system and hitherto unseen (or repressed) foreign policy alternatives suddenly come into view. Being Rome or Britain no longer defines the full menu of options. Gracefully adjusting to the reality of being one great power among several—which events will oblige the United States to do in any case—becomes a possibility.

Alas, the likelihood of any such reevaluation occurring anytime soon is small. This is true not only because those wielding
power in Washington oppose any change in the status quo but
because the American people can't or won't make the effort.

Here's why. However packaged, the three yeses all imply collective obligation. That's something a culture in thrall to celebrities,
geeks, and warriors cannot abide.

In the early 1970s, a failed war reinforced by a radical shift in
culture persuaded Americans to jettison the tradition of the
citizen-soldier. In creating the all-volunteer force, Richard Nixon
accurately interpreted the popular will.

Forty years later, the mournful consequences of this decision
continue to pile up. Not least among them is a proclivity for wars
that are, if anything, even more misguided and counterproduc-
tive than Vietnam was. Yet this time around, a collective refusal
even to acknowledge those consequences takes precedence over
corrective action. The warriors may be brave, but the people are
timid. So where courage is most needed, passivity prevails, exqui-
sitely expressed (and sanctimoniously justified) in the omnipres-
ent call to "support the troops."

CODA

The American people have rarely devoted more than passing
attention to their relationship with their military. In recent decades,
they have ignored the subject altogether. In an earlier day, however, the issue did command the attention of at least some American soldiers. Prominent among them was George C. Marshall.

General Marshall understood that when it came to basic military policy, the central question was not whether the United States
could create armed forces sufficient to protect itself and its most
important interests, but whether it would do so in ways consistent
with the aspirations expressed in foundational documents such as

the Declaration of Independence and the Constitution. The real challenge, in other words, lay in harmonizing the imperatives of defense with the values of democracy.

Marshall believed such a harmonization not only possible but necessary. As army chief of staff during World War II, he personally modeled what this implied on the part of senior military officers assigned duties at the summit of power. In his own conduct, Marshall subordinated himself without reservation or complaint to civilian authority. He resolutely avoided any action carrying the slightest taint of partisanship—hence, for example, his principled refusal even to vote in national elections.[12] To emphasize that his loyalty (and that of the officer corps as a whole) was to the country and not any particular individual, party, or administration, he avoided undue familiarity or false intimacy with senior civilian officials. He also insisted that those to whom he reported—the president and the secretary of war—acknowledge and respect his own authority over matters falling within the purview of the military profession. He tenaciously defended the prerogatives of the officer corps, resisting inappropriate civilian incursions into the military sphere.[13]

Yet determined as he was to maintain both the principle of civilian control and the status of the military profession, Marshall understood that these actions alone would not ensure a satisfactory civil-military relationship. More important than the interaction between senior officers and senior civilian officials, in his estimation, was the bond between the people and their army. Marshall believed that the two should be one, with the citizen-soldier tradition the key to ensuring this essential unity. Although devoted to the military's professional ethic of "duty, honor, country," Marshall insisted that the citizen-soldier—not the regular—should form the basis of the American military system, whether in times of war or peace.

With World War II still undecided, but the United States on the cusp of becoming the world's leading power, Marshall warned against the temptation to create a standing army, its ranks filled with professionals instead of citizen-soldiers. "There are two types of organization through which the manpower of a nation may be developed," he wrote in August 1944.

> One of these is the standing army type. . . . This is the system of Germany and Japan. It produces highly efficient armies. But it is open to political objections. . . . It, therefore, has no place among the institutions of a modern democratic state based on the conception of government by the people.
>
> The second type of military institution . . . is based upon the conception of a professional peace establishment (no larger than necessary to meet normal peacetime requirements) to be reinforced in time of emergency by organized units drawn from a citizen army reserve, effectively organized for this purpose in time of peace. . . . This is the type of army which President Washington proposed to the First Congress as one of the essential foundations of the new American Republic. . . . It will therefore be made the basis for all plans for a post-war peace establishment.[14]

In his final report as chief of staff, Marshall returned to this theme. "War has been defined by a people who have thought a lot about it—the Germans," he wrote. The German view held that "an invincible offensive military force . . . could win any political argument."

> This is the doctrine Hitler carried to the verge of complete success. It is the doctrine of Japan. It is a criminal doctrine, and like other forms of crime, it has cropped up again and again since

man began to live with his neighbors in communities and nations. There has long been an effort to outlaw war for exactly the same reason that man has outlawed murder. But the law prohibiting murder does not of itself prevent murder. It must be enforced. The enforcing power, however, must be maintained on a strictly democratic basis. There must not be a large standing army subject to the behest of a group of schemers. The citizen-soldier is the guarantee against such a misuse of power.[15]

Writing as the preeminent American exponent of genuine military professionalism, Marshall could hardly have stated his admonition in clearer terms: to abandon the tradition of the citizen-soldier, seeking to create an invincible offensive force able to win any argument, was to open the door to schemers pursuing criminal policies. Sadly, this describes what Americans have allowed to occur in our own day.

The all-volunteer force is not a blessing. It has become a blight. Americans can, of course, choose to pretend otherwise, but those choosing such a course cannot be said to love their country. Nor can they be said to care about the well-being of those sent to fight on the country's behalf.

NOTES

INTRODUCTION

1. Bernard Fall recounts the fate of G. M. 100 in chapter 9 of his classic book *Street Without Joy* (Harrisburg, Pa., 1961).

2. "G. I. Charged with CO Slaying," *Pacific Stars & Stripes*, February 2, 1971.

3. George W. Bush, ""President Bush Discusses Freedom in Iraq and Middle East," November 6, 2003, http://georgewbush-whitehouse.archives.gov/news/releases/2003/11/20031106-2.html, accessed October 9, 2012.

4. At least two additional questions also figure in determining the content of democracy. *What* is the operative meaning of freedom? And *to whom* are the privileges of freedom permitted?

1. PEOPLE'S WAR

1. Franklin D. Roosevelt, "Four Freedoms Speech," January 6, 1941, http://www.americanrhetoric.com/speeches/fdrthefourfreedoms.htm, accessed July 26, 2011. In concrete terms, FDR explained, this translated into "economic understandings which will secure to every nation a healthy peacetime life for its inhabitants—everywhere in the world." Yet as interpreted by the illustrator Norman Rockwell, "Freedom from Want" signified a happy American family gathered around a dining room table, piled high with all the bounty associated with the American tradition of Thanksgiving. By implica-

tion, *freedom* in this context meant not global free trade agreements but unfettered personal consumption.

2. William L. O'Neill, *A Democracy at War: America's Fight at Home and Abroad in World War II* (New York, 1993), pp. vii, 434.

3. Quoted in Keith Eiler, *Mobilizing America: Robert P. Patterson and the War Effort, 1940–1945* (Ithaca, N.Y., 1997), p. 282. Patterson was testifying before the Senate Committee on Military Affairs.

4. Roosevelt, "Four Freedoms Speech."

5. NFL players Jack Lummus and Maurice Britt won the Medal of Honor, the nation's highest award for valor. Lummus received the award posthumously. http://www.profootballhof.com/history/general/war/worldwar2/page2.jsp, accessed July 3, 2007.

6. U.S. Military Academy Library, "Graduates—World War II Casualties," spreadsheet in the author's possession, received July 28, 2011.

7. John Hersey, *Into the Valley: Marines at Guadalcanal* (New York, 1943), p. 43.

8. James Gould Cozzens, *Guard of Honor* (New York, 1948), p. 275.

9. Richard R. Lingeman, *Don't You Know There's a War On?* (New York, 1970), p. 208.

10. James A. Wechsler, "The Liberal's Vote and '48," *Commentary*, September 1947, pp. 217–18.

11. The German U-boat campaign threatened to sever the link between the arsenal of democracy and the actual fighting front. Hence the imperative of winning the so-called Battle of the Atlantic, which the Allies succeeded in doing by 1944.

12. George C. Marshall, "West Point and the Citizen Army" (May 29, 1942), in *Selected Speeches and Statements of General of the Army George C. Marshall*, ed. H. A. DeWeerd (Washington, D.C., 1945), p. 204.

13. Interview with Marshall, July 25, 1949, quoted in Maurice Matloff, *Strategic Planning for Coalition Warfare, 1943–1944* (Washington, D.C., 1959), p. 5.

14. Quoted in Mark A. Stoler, *Allies and Adversaries: The Joint Chiefs of Staff, the Grand Alliance, and U.S. Strategy in World War II* (Chapel Hill, N.C., 2006), pp. 85, 99.

15. Ibid., p. 115.

16. Williamson Murray and Allan R. Millett, *A War to Be Won: Fighting the Second World War* (Cambridge, Mass., 2000), p. 558.

17. H. P. Willmott, *The Second World War in the Far East* (Washington, D.C., 1999), p. 34.

18. Ibid., p. 128.

19. Marshall, *Selected Speeches*, p. 36.

20. Paul A. C. Koistinen, *Arsenal of World War II: The Political Economy of American Warfare, 1940–1945* (Lawrence, Kans., 2004), p. 498.

21. Harold Vatter, *The U.S. Economy in World War II* (New York, 1985), p. 143.

22. Richard Polenberg, *War and Society: The United States, 1941–1945* (Philadelphia, 1972), p. 94.

23. Koistinen, *Arsenal,* p. 430.

2. THE GREAT DECOUPLING

1. Wendell Berry first posed this crucially important question in March 2003. See his "A Citizen's Response to the National Security Strategy of the United States of America," http://www.quietspaces.com/wendellberry.html, accessed December 26, 2011.

2. Franklin D. Roosevelt, Fireside Chat, December 9, 1941, http://www.mhric.org/fdr/chat19.html.

3. *The 9/11 Commission Report* (Washington, D.C., 2004), p. 39.

4. http://www.budweiser.com/en/world-of-budweiser/mlb/default.aspx#/en/world-of-budweiser/mlb/index, accessed July 11, 2011.

5. http://www.millerhighlife.com/high-life-experiences/, accessed July 11, 2011.

6. Not all of these public relations stunts panned out as planned. In 2012, a major insurance company joined with the National Football League to organize a "Million Fan Salute." The idea was to "Unite with the NFL to salute the military." The "NFL cities that collect[ed] the most salutes" would "earn rewards for their local military community," courtesy of the insurance company. The nature of the rewards was not specified. Unfortunately, when the voting closed, only 142,916 fans had weighed in, so the results fell well short of a million. http://millionfansalute.com/, accessed December 5, 2012.

7. Ron Suskind, *The Price of Loyalty: George W. Bush, the White House, and the Education of Paul O'Neill* (New York, 2004), p. 291.

3. TALLYING UP

1. Bill Clinton, "Remarks by the President at America's Millennium Gala," December 31, 1999, http://clinton4.nara.gov/WH/New/html/20000104.html.

2. Thomas E. Woods Jr., *Meltdown: A Free Market Look at Why the Stock Market Collapsed, the Economy Tanked, and Government Bailouts Will Make Things Worse* (Washington, D.C., 2009); Gretchen Morgenson and Joshua Rosner, *Reckless Endangerment: How Outsized Ambition, Greed, and Corruption Led to Economic Armageddon* (New York, 2011); Joseph E. Stiglitz, *Freefall: America, Free Markets, and the Sinking of the World Economy* (New York, 2010); Barry James Dyke, *The Pirates of Manhattan: Systematically Plundering the American Consumer and How to Protect Against It* (2007); John Perkins, *Hoodwinked: An Economic Hit Man Reveals Why the World Financial Markets Imploded—and What We Need to Do to Remake Them* (New York, 2009); David Faber, *And Then the Roof Caved In: How Wall Street's Greed and Stupidity Brought Capitalism to Its Knees* (Hoboken, N.J. 2010); Chris Harman, *Zombie Capitalism: Global Crisis and the Relevance of Marx* (Chicago, 2010); Les Leopold, *The Looting of America: How Wall Street's Game of Fantasy Finance Destroyed Our Jobs, Pensions, and Prosperity—and What We Can Do About It* (White River Junction, Vt., 2009); William D. Cohan, *House of Cards: A Tale of Hubris and Wretched Excess on Wall Street* (New York, 2010); Barry Ritholtz, *Bailout Nation: How Greed and Easy Money Corrupted Wall Street and Shook the World Economy* (Hoboken, N.J., 2009); Menzie D. Chinn and Jeffry A. Frieden, *Lost Decades: The Making of America's Debt Crisis and the Long Recovery* (New York, 2011); Richard Heinberg, *The End of Growth: Adapting to Our New Economic Reality* (Gabriola Island, British Columbia, 2011); Thomas L. Friedman and Michael Mandelbaum, *That Used to Be Us: How America Fell Behind in the World It Invented—and How We Can Come Back* (New York, 2011).

3. "7.9 Million Jobs Lost—Many Forever," July 2, 2010, http://money.cnn.com/2010/07/02/news/economy/jobs_gone_forever/index.htm, accessed December 30, 2011.

4. Pallavi Gogoi, "The Jobless Effect," July 16, 2010, http://www.dailyfinance.com/2010/07/16/what-is-the-real-unemployment-rate/, accessed December 31, 2011.

5. Michael Greenstone and Adam Looney, "The Great Recession's Toll on Long-Term Unemployment," November 5, 2010, http://www.brookings.edu/opinions/2010/1105_jobs_greenstone_looney.aspx, accessed December 31, 2011.

6. Catherine Rampell, "Career Shift Often Means Drop in Living Standards," *New York Times*, December 31, 2010.

7. By 2010, 15 percent of Americans were officially classified as poor, and 14 percent of adults relied on food stamps. Cynthia Enloe and Joni Seager, *The Real State of America Atlas* (New York, 2011), pp. 54–55.

8. Sabrina Tavernise, "Soaring Poverty Casts Spotlight on 'Lost Decade,'" *New York Times*, September 13, 2011.

9. Joseph E. Stieglitz, "Of the 1%, By the 1%, For the 1%," *Vanity Fair*, May 2011, http://www.vanityfair.com/society/features/2011/05/top-one-percent-201105, accessed January 7, 2012.

10. Geoffrey Perret, *A Country Made by War: From the Revolution to Vietnam—The Story of America's Rise to Power* (New York, 1989).

11. Max Boot, "Afghanistan—The 'Who Cares?' War," *Wall Street Journal*, August 29, 2012.

12. Among developed countries, the United States ranks second in the percentage of children living in relative poverty, trailing only Romania. UNICEF, *Measuring Child Poverty*, May 2012, p. 3.

13. At present approximately 842,000 Americans are homeless on any given day, with some 3.5 million Americans experiencing homelessness over the course of a year. National Resource and Training Center on Homelessness and Mental Illness, "Who Is Homeless?" http://web.archive.org/web/20070510103756/http://www.nrchmi.samhsa.gov/facts/facts_question_2.asp, accessed August 29, 2012.

14. Jason DeParle and Sabrina Tavernise, "For Women Under Thirty, Most Births Occur Outside Marriage," *New York Times*, February 17, 2012.

15. Eating disorders affect up to 24 million Americans. "Eating Disorder Statistics," National Association of Anorexia Nervosa and Associated Disorders, http://www.anad.org/get-information/about-eating-disorders/eating-disorders-statistics/, accessed August 29, 2012.

16. "Over one-third of all Americans today are obese, up from 15% in 1980. During that same period, the obesity rate of American children ages 2–19 tripled, reaching 16.9% in 2011. In only a single state (Colorado) does the obesity rate today fall below 20%. In ten states, the obesity rate exceeds 30%." Trust for America's Health, *F as in Fat: How Obesity Threatens America's Future* (2011), http://healthyamericans.org/assets/files/TFAH2011FasInFat10.pdf, accessed January 2, 2012.

17. Drug overdoses "now represent the leading cause of accidental death in the United States, having overtaken motor vehicle accidents for the first time on record." Kevin A. Sabet, "Overdosing on Extremism," *New York Times*, January 1, 2012.

18. Enloe and Seager, *Real State of America Atlas*, p. 89. In 2010, the collective personal debt of the American people exceeded the total GDP. Credit card debt alone averaged $16,000 per household.

19. The U.S. Department of Agriculture estimates that "food insecurity"

affected some 50 million Americans in 2010, meaning that they were members of a household that during the course of the year "lacked money and other resources for food." USDA Economic Research Service, *Household Food Security in the United States in 2010*, September 2011.

20. The United States today has the highest incarceration rate in the world, the total U.S. prison population having quadrupled in just the past three decades. In 2009, the U.S. prison population was nearly 2.3 million, with over 7.2 million U.S. residents either behind bars, on probation, or on parole. The current incarceration rate is 5.5 times larger than the previous spike coinciding with the Great Depression. Bureau of Justice Statistics, "Total Correctional Population," 2009, http://bjs.ojp.usdoj.gov/index.cfm?ty=tp&tid=11.

21. Arguably, the military itself has benefited from the Great Recession in this one sense: civilian economic distress boosts military recruiting. For the young and able-bodied, the armed services have jobs available.

22. Jonathan Turley, "10 Reasons the United States Is No Longer the Land of the Free," *Washington Post*, January 13, 2012.

23. Ezra Klein, "Why Do Harvard Kids Head to Wall Street," *Washington Post*, April 23, 2010, http://voices.washingtonpost.com/ezra-klein/2010/04/why_do_harvard_kids_head_to_wa.html, accessed January 11, 2012.

24. The Pat Tillman experience stands out because it is that: a striking exception. Tillman's death has not inspired other professional athletes to enlist. For those hungering for a bit of vicarious experience, of course, there is always "reality TV." In 2012, a short-lived series called *Stars Earn Stripes* offered marginal celebrities and former jocks keen to play at soldiering a chance to satisfy that urge without them actually having to enlist. Hosted by the retired army General Wesley Clark, *Stars Earn Stripes* put the likes of Nick Lachey (ex-husband of faded pop phenom) and Todd Palin (current husband of a faded political phenom) into battle dress and simulated combat, thereby ostensibly paying tribute to those who actually do serve and fight. "Gun porn," the *New Republic* called it. "Pretty interesting, pretty tough, pretty awesome" was how General Clark saw it. Laura Bennett, "General Failure: The Bizarre World of Wesley Clark's New Reality Show," *New Republic*, August 15, 2012.

25. As one former officer wrote, "The public apathy that has long characterized our involvement in this war is obviously, in large part, the result of an all-volunteer military force that has left the 99 percent blissfully unaware of the daily triumphs and tragedies that mark the lives of many of their fellow citizens a world away." Will Bardenwerper, "U.S. Soldiers at War: The Forgotten One Percent," *Washington Post*, November 10, 2011.

4. AMERICA'S ARMY

1. The phrase is Ralph Waldo Emerson's, from his 1837 poem "Concord Hymn." In 1999, President Bill Clinton selected "Concord Hymn" as his choice for the national "Favorite Poem" project. http://www.youtube.com/watch?v=q-XViGsKwNY&feature=related.

2. Colonel Robert D. Heinl Jr., "The Collapse of the Armed Forces," *Armed Forces Journal*, June 7, 1971, pp. 30–38.

3. Robert D. Heinl Jr., "The U.S. Army in Search of Itself," *Saturday Evening Post*, August 1974, p. 40.

4. At Memorial Day ceremonies in 2012, marking (somewhat arbitrarily) the fiftieth anniversary of the beginning of the Vietnam War, President Barack Obama put his official imprimatur on this remembered ill-treatment of Vietnam vets. "You came home," Obama told the vets in the crowd, and "were denigrated when you should have been celebrated." The treatment accorded Vietnam veterans, he continued, had been "a national shame, a disgrace that never should have happened." "Remarks by the President at the Commemoration Ceremony of the Fiftieth Anniversary of the Vietnam War," May 28, 2012, http://www.whitehouse.gov/the-press-office/2012/05/28/remarks-president-commemoration-ceremony-50th-anniversary-vietnam-war, accessed May 29, 2012.

5. Karl H. Purnell, "The Army's Kangaroo Courts," *Nation*, April 7, 1969, p. 434.

6. Ward Just, *Military Men* (New York, 1970), pp. 4–5.

7. Colonel David H. Hackworth, "A Soldier's Disgust," *Harper's*, July 1972, p. 74.

8. "Disorder in the Ranks," *Time*, August 19, 1971, p. 21. In an internal army report evaluating the sources of indiscipline in the army's ranks, officers faulted American society for the problems besetting the army. "Virtually all commanders," the report stated, according to *Time*, "place strong emphasis on permissiveness within American society as being a primary cause of disciplinary breakdown. The point is made that the draftee, the draft-induced enlistee and many of our junior officers have been influenced by permissive homes, permissive schools and permissive courts."

9. The literature on war resistance within the ranks of the military is both extensive and impassioned. For a succinct account, see Matthew Rinaldi, "The Olive Drab Rebels: Military Organizing During the Vietnam Era," *Radical America*, May–June 1974, pp. 17–52.

10. For a sample of newspapers, see "Photos and Documents, GI

Underground Newspapers," http://depts.washington.edu/antiwar/photo_
gipapers.php, accessed March 8, 2012. The Web site includes digitized copies
of several newspapers, among them *Counterpoint, Fed Up*, and the *G. I. Voice*.
Front-page headlines give a flavor of the contents: "AWOLs Soar," "Racism
Exposed," "Riot Rocks Fort Ord," "Nixon Desperate," "Jane Fonda Banned
From Fort," and "How To Get Over."

11. Peter Barnes, "The Presidio 'Mutiny,'" *New Republic*, July 5, 1969, pp.
21–25; John V. H. Dippel, "Going Nowhere Through Channels," *New Republic*,
May 22, 1971, pp. 13–17.

12. Just, *Military Men*, p. 62.

13. Subcommittee to Investigate the Administration of the Internal
Security Act and Other Internal Security Laws, *Organized Subversion in the
U.S. Armed Forces* (Washington, D.C., 1976), part 1, pp. 2, 5, 17.

14. Eugene Linden, "Fragging and Other Withdrawal Symptoms," *Saturday Review*, January 8, 1972, pp. 12–17.

15. "Black Explosions in West Germany," *Time*, September 21, 1970,
p. 36.

16. "Forgotten Seventh Army," *Time*, October 4, 1971, p. 18.

17. Leonard Gross, "Our Uptight Troops in Europe," *Look*, September 8,
1970, pp. 14–19.

18. Subcommittee to Investigate the Administration of the Internal
Security Act and Other Internal Security Laws, *Organized Subversion in the
U.S. Armed Forces*, part 1, appendix 2, pp. 2–3.

19. Beth Bailey, *America's Army: Making the All-Volunteer Force* (Cambridge, Mass., 2009), p. xi.

20. Quoted in Aaron Friedberg, *In the Shadow of the Garrison State:
America's Anti-Statism and Its Cold War Grand Strategy* (Princeton, N.J.,
2000), pp. 192, 195.

21. *The Report of the President's Commission on an All-Volunteer Armed
Force*, February 1970, http://www.rand.org/pubs/monographs/MG265/images/
webS0243.pdf, accessed March 10, 2012. The commission was more com-
monly known as the Gates Commission. The final monthly draft call
occurred in December 1972, with those selected reporting for duty in June
1973.

22. Heinl, "Army in Search of Itself," p. 33.

23. Quoted in Michael Klare, "Can the Army Survive VOLAR?" *Common-
weal*, January 18, 1974, p. 387.

24. Robert K. Griffith Jr., *The U.S. Army's Transition to the All-Volunteer
Force* (Washington, D.C., 1997), p. 25.

25. William C. Westmoreland, "Talking About the Army," *Vital Speeches of the Day* (May 15, 1969), p. 451.

26. For U.S. military pay scales going back to 1949, see "Historical Military Pay Rates," http://www.military.com/benefits/content/military-pay/charts/historical-military-pay-rates.html, accessed April 10, 2012. When I received my commission in June 1969, a second lieutenant's monthly pay was $343.

27. "Chickenshit," writes Fussell, "refers . . . to behavior that makes military life worse than it need be: petty harassment of the weak by the strong; open scrimmage for power and authority and prestige; sadism thinly disguised as necessary discipline; a constant 'paying off of old scores'; and insistence on the letter rather than the spirit of ordinances. Chickenshit is so called—instead of horse- or bull- or elephant shit—because it is small-minded and ignoble and takes the trivial seriously. Chickenshit can be recognized instantly because it never has anything to do with winning the war." Paul Fussell, *Wartime: Understanding and Behavior in the Second World War* (New York, 1989), p. 80.

28. The definition comes from the *Shorter Oxford English Dictionary*, 6th ed. (New York, 2007), vol. 2, p. 2911.

29. The 1953 motion picture *From Here to Eternity* and the 1951 novel on which the movie was based vividly illustrate this aspect of a soldier's existence. The novel's author, James Jones, refers to this as "Fatigue," writing that "the knowledge of the unendingness and of the repetitious uselessness, the do it up so it can be done again" made such duty "not only fatiguing but degrading." *From Here to Eternity*, chap. 8.

30. "G. I. Dormitories," *Time*, March 26, 1973, p. 98. See also Jonathan Schell, "The Enlisted Man," *New Yorker*, March 17, 1973, p. 33.

5. COMES THE REVOLUTION

1. Charles C. Moskos, "Success Story: Blacks in the Military," *Atlantic Monthly*, May 1986, http://www.theatlantic.com/past/docs/unbound/flashbks/black/moskos.htm, accessed April 8, 2012.

2. Even during the Vietnam era, the army officer corps was less than 3 percent black. Ibid.

3. Frederic Ellis Davison was promoted to brigadier general in 1968, ultimately retiring as a major general in 1974.

4. For an appreciation of the racial climate of the time, see Wallace Terry, "Black Power in Vietnam," *Time*, September 19, 1969.

5. Jeffrey K. Toomer, "A Corps of Many Colors: The Evolution of the Minority Recruiting Effort at the United States Military Academy," unpublished research paper, November 14, 1997, p. 5.

6. The cadet company to which I was assigned for four years during the latter half of the 1960s contained an equal number of blacks and Jews—one of each.

7. James Feron, "Blacks in a Long Gray Line," *New York Times*, June 2, 1991.

8. I am grateful to the serving officer who provided me with this data.

9. Charles Moskos and John Sibley Butler, *All That We Can Be: Black Leadership and Racial Integration the Army Way* (New York, 1996). The quote comes off the book's back cover.

10. A. C. Showers, "Rocking the Boat: Women Enter Military Academies," unpublished paper, University of Colorado at Boulder, April 22, 2008.

11. Jane Gross, "Sergeant Major Gets One-Step Demotion But No Time in Jail," *New York Times*, March 17, 1998. At roughly the same time, the army charged the senior noncommissioned officer in U.S. Army Europe with "forcible sodomy, kidnapping, indecent assault and maltreatment" of a female subordinate. David Stout, "The Army's Top NCO in Europe Is Charged with Sexual Assault," *New York Times*, October 23, 1999.

12. Paul Richter, "Army Demotes by 1 Rank Retired General in Sex Case," *Los Angeles Times*, September 3, 1999.

13. Tom Bowman, "Army Sends Message, Strip General's Rank for Conduct," *Baltimore Sun*, November 17, 1999.

14. Christopher Marquis, "General Seeks to Retire as Charges Are Supported," *New York Times*, July 8, 2000.

15. Kennedy's memoir *Generally Speaking* appeared in 2002. Two years later, she addressed the Democratic National Convention that nominated Senator John Kerry for the presidency.

16. For examples of this literature, see Brian Mitchell, *Women in the Military: Flirting with Disaster* (Washington, D.C., 1998), and Stephanie Gutmann, *The Kinder, Gentler Military: Can America's Gender-Neutral Fighting Force Still Win Wars?* (New York, 2000).

17. James Webb, "The War on the Military Culture," *Weekly Standard*, January 20, 1997.

18. Dennis A. Williams with Eleanor Clift, "This Woman's Army," *Newsweek*, October 20, 1975.

19. The most famous female POW of the Iraq War was Private Jessica Lynch, who for a brief moment became, as the journalist Evan Wright put it,

the war's Helen of Troy. But others included Shoshana Johnson and Lori Ann Piestewa. Lynch and Johnson survived and wrote books about their experience. Piestewa died in captivity. Evan Wright, *Generation Kill: Devil Dogs, Iceman, Captain America, and the New Face of American War* (New York, 2004), p. 222.

20. In 2007, Sergeant Leigh Ann Hester became the first woman since World War II to receive the Silver Star. Others followed.

21. "Military Casualty Information," http://siadapp.dmdc.osd.mil/personnel/CASUALTY/castop.htm, accessed May 4, 2012. Of the total, eighty-nine were army soldiers, with the remainder coming from the other services.

22. By comparison, the Korean War claimed the lives of eighteen military women and Vietnam eight, even though the total of Americans killed in those two wars vastly exceeded the number lost in Iraq. "Korean War Casualty Information," http://www.koreanwar-educator.org/topics/casualties/p_casualties_women_kia.htm, and "American Women Who Died in the Vietnam War," http://www.countryjoe.com/nightingale/sisters.htm, both accessed May 4, 2012.

23. Iraq War fatalities amounted to 4,475 U.S. military personnel, with 3,517 killed in action and 958 deaths due to nonhostile causes. Another 32,225 soldiers were wounded in action. "Operation Iraqi Freedom (OIF) U. S. Casualty Status," http://www.defense.gov/news/casualty.pdf, accessed May 4, 2012.

24. As of mid-May 2012, 31 of 1,960 fatalities suffered by U.S. forces in Afghanistan were women. http://icasualties.org/OEF/Fatalities.aspx, accessed May 7, 2012.

25. Juliette Kayyem, "The Military's Persistent Gender Divide," *Boston Globe*, April 23, 2012.

26. Petula Dvorak, "Why Army Women Are Demanding the Right to Fight—and Die—in Combat," *Washington Post*, May 28, 2012.

27. James Dao, "Servicewomen File Suit Over Direct Combat Ban," *New York Times*, November 27, 2012.

28. Lolita C. Baldor, "Army Reviews Whether Women Can Go to Ranger School," May 16, 2012, http://www.kgwn.tv/story/18437747/army-reviews-whether-women-can-go-to-ranger-school, accessed May 25, 2012.

29. As the army's institutional commitment to gender equality has grown, so too has the prevalence of sexual assault within the ranks, increasing 64 percent between 2006 and 2011, for example. With few exceptions, the victims are female. Whether expanding the number and role of women in the army fosters this epidemic or creates conditions that will lead to its elimination remains to be seen. Anna Mulrine, "Pentagon Report: Sexual

Assault in the Military Up Dramatically," *Christian Science Monitor,* January 19, 2012.

30. Elisabeth Bumiller and Thom Shanker, "Pentagon Is Set to Lift Combat Ban for Women," *New York Times,* January 23, 2013.

31. Dvorak, "Why Women Are Demanding the Right to Fight—and Die—in Combat."

32. Joel Connelly and Scott Sunde, "Clinton Runs Hard in State," *Seattle Post-Intelligencer,* July 27, 1992.

33. Thomas L. Friedman, "Clinton to Open Military's Ranks to Homosexuals," *New York Times,* November 12, 1992.

34. Eric Schmitt, "In Promising to End Ban on Homosexuals, Clinton Is Confronting a Wall of Tradition," *New York Times,* November 11, 1992.

35. Eric Schmitt, "Joint Chiefs Fighting Clinton Plan to Allow Homosexuals in Military," *New York Times,* January 23, 1993.

36. Editorial, "Who's in Charge of the Military?" *New York Times,* January 26, 1993.

37. Emily Bazelon, "Don't Ask, Don't Tell, Don't Rock the Boat," *Slate,* May 10, 2010.

38. Palm Center publications are available at the center's Web site: http://www.palmcenter.org/publications/all.

39. "More Gay Linguists Discharged Than First Thought," *MSNBC.com,* January 13, 2005, http://www.msnbc.msn.com/id/6824206/ns/us_news-security /t/report-more-gay-linguistsdischarged-first-thought/, accessed June 5, 2012.

40. Karen DeYoung, "Colin Powell Now Says Gays Should Be Allowed to Serve Openly in Military," *Washington Post,* February 4, 2010.

41. Thomas E. Ricks, "Petraeus: Gay Soldiers No Biggie," ForeignPolicy .com, February 22, 2010, http://ricks.foreignpolicy.com/posts/2010/02/22/ petraeus_gay_soldiers_no_biggie, accessed June 5, 2012.

42. Mark Thompson, "Why Is the Military Polling the Troops about Gays?" *Time,* July 12, 2010.

43. The figure comes from the Web site of the Servicemembers Legal Defense Network, http://www.sldn.org/pages/about-dadt, accessed June 5, 2012.

44. Cid Standifer, "Survey: DADT Repeal Has Less Impact Than Expected," *Marine Corps Times,* March 12, 2012. With the promotion of Colonel Tammy S. Smith to brigadier general in August 2012, the army gained its first openly gay flag officer. A milestone in the eyes of some, the event was devoid of controversy. Matthew Wald, "Woman Becomes First Openly Gay General," *New York Times,* August 12, 2012.

45. Phil Stewart, "Pentagon: No Impact from Ending Gay Ban," *News-Daily*, May 10, 2012.

46. "After 'Don't Ask, Don't Tell,'" *Harvard Magazine*, December 2010.

47. One wonders how long the Pentagon's authority even in this arena will last. Take the case of an otherwise able-bodied person who is confined to a wheelchair but aspires to become a drone pilot: on what basis does the air force deny that person his or her right to serve?

6. SEARCHING FOR DRAGONS TO SLAY

1. The characterization is that of Brian Linn, whose forthcoming book will provide a social and cultural history of the army during the interval between the Korea and Vietnam Wars.

2. For a more detailed account of the army's reorientation on the Soviet threat after Vietnam, see Andrew J. Bacevich, *The New American Militarism: How Americans Are Seduced by War* (New York, updated edition, 2013), chap. 2.

3. General Gordon R. Sullivan and Michael V. Harper, *Hope Is Not a Method* (New York, 1997), p. 3.

4. Ibid., p. 5.

5. General Gordon R. Sullivan, "Moving into the 21st Century," *Military Review*, July 1993, p. 3. That expectation proved correct. When the Cold War ended, the army had approximately 780,000 active duty troops. Twenty years later, on the eve of 9/11, there were 480,000.

6. TRADOC Pamphlet 525-5, *Force XXI Operations* (August 1, 1994), chap. 4. This publication by U.S. Army Training and Doctrine Command provided the army's blueprint for post–Cold War reform.

7. General Gordon R. Sullivan and Colonel James M. Dubik, "Land Warfare in the 21st Century," *Military Review*, September 1993, p. 18.

8. General Dennis Reimer, "Soldiers Are Our Credentials," *Military Review*, September–October 1995, p. 14.

9. General Fredrick M. Franks Jr., "Full-Dimensional Operations," *Military Review*, December 1993, p. 8.

10. Ibid., pp. 5, 8.

11. Lieutenant General John H. Tilelli Jr., "Force Projection: Essential to Army Doctrine," *Military Review*, January 1994, p. 21.

12. Sullivan, "Moving into the 21st Century," p. 4.

13. Colonel Herbert F. Harback and Colonel Ulrich H. Keller, "Learning Leader XXI," *Military Review*, May–June 1995, pp. 31–32.

14. General J. H. Binford Peay III, "Building America's Power Projection Army," *Military Review,* July 1994, p. 14.

15. General Carl E. Vuono, "National Strategy and the Army of the 1990s," *Parameters,* Summer 1991, p. 11.

16. Sullivan and Dubik, "Land Warfare," p. 14.

17. General Carl E. Vuono, "Training and the Army of the 1990s," *Military Review,* January 1991, p. 4.

18. Warsaw Pact war plans made public after the Cold War make this clear. John O'Sullivan, "Europe's Nuclear War That Might Have Been," *San Diego Union-Tribune,* December 25, 2005. The article discusses a 1979 Warsaw Pact planning exercise called "Seven Days to the River Rhine."

19. Vuono, "National Strategy," p. 12.

20. Sullivan and Dubik, "Land Warfare," pp. 18–19.

21. General Carl E. Vuono, "Professionalism and the Army of the 1990s," *Military Review,* April 1990, p. 2.

22. Lieutenant General Frederic J. Brown, "The Uncertain Path," *Military Review,* June 1990, pp. 3–4. Army leaders established the truly stupendous goal of being able to deploy "a five-division corps with support (more than 150,000 soldiers) anywhere in the world within 75 days." Tilelli, "Force Projection Essential to Army Doctrine," p. 17.

23. General Gordon R. Sullivan, "Power Projection and the Challenges of Regionalism," *Parameters,* Summer 1993, pp. 11, 15.

24. Peay, "Building America's Power Projection Army," p. 6.

25. General Gordon R. Sullivan, "A Trained and Ready Army: The Way Ahead," *Military Review,* November 1991, p. 3.

26. General Gordon R. Sullivan, "Doctrine: A Guide to the Future," *Military Review,* February 1992, p. 3.

27. FM 100-5, *Operations,* June 1993, pp. 2–6.

28. General Gordon R. Sullivan, "Delivering Decisive Victory," *Military Review,* September 1992, p. 3.

29. Sullivan, "Trained and Ready," p. 5.

30. General Gordon R. Sullivan, "Ulysses S. Grant and America's Power Projection Army," *Military Review,* January 1994, p. 8.

31. General Gordon R. Sullivan, "A Vision for the Future," *Military Review,* May–June 1995, pp. 8, 13.

32. Sullivan, "Moving into the 21st Century," p. 3.

33. The name of the battle derives from the location where it occurred as expressed by the Universal Transverse Mercator (UTM) grid system.

34. For the U.S. commander's firsthand account, see Captain H. R.

McMaster, "The Battle of 73 Easting," undated, Donovan Research Library, Fort Benning, Georgia.

35. By studying the battle in granular detail, the army reconstructed it on a minute-by-minute basis and then converted the action into a sophisticated computer simulation. W. M. Christenson and Robert A. Zirkle, "73 Easting Battle Replication—a Janus Combat Simulation," September 1992. This was a study conducted under the auspices of the Institute for Defense Analyses.

36. TRADOC Pamphlet 525-5, chap. 3.

37. Lieutenant General Paul E. Menoher Jr., "Force XXI: Redesigning the Army Through Warfighting Experiments," *Military Intelligence Professional Bulletin* (undated [1996]).

38. Regarding Somalia, Sullivan believed, "We did fine tactically. Probably operationally. Strategically, because of what happened in Mogadishu, it clearly wasn't a loss . . . . [O]ut in the countryside we made great progress." Colonel John R. Dabrowski, ed., *An Oral History of General Gordon R. Sullivan* (Carlisle, Penn., 2002), p. 266.

39. Andrew J. Bacevich, "The United States in Iraq: Terminating an Interminable War," in *Between War and Peace: How America Ends Its Wars,* ed. Matthew Moten (New York, 2011), pp. 302–22.

40. One might argue that the first shots in this conflict were actually fired years before 1990, the War for the Persian Gulf having been touched off in 1980 when Iraq invaded Iran, with the United States becoming a de facto ally of Saddam Hussein's Iraq.

41. David Jackson and Aamer Madhani, "Obama: Full Withdrawal from Iraq by Jan. 1," *USAToday,* October 21, 2011.

42. One caveat to this judgment: if, as some critics have charged, Iraq's oil reserves provided the actual motive for invading that country, the war shows signs of belated, if costly, success. By 2012, Iraqi petroleum production was (finally) increasing, with the removal of Saddam Hussein's regime having enhanced the access and investment opportunities of foreign oil companies. Javier Blas, "Iraq's Oil Output Overtakes Iran," *Washington Post,* August 10, 2012.

43. Rather than obsessing about 73 Easting, the army would have been better served to study the negotiations that terminated Operation Desert Storm, badly botched by army generals in Washington and the field. Here was raw material for an eminently instructive simulation.

44. I refer here to the 1996 attack on the U.S. Air Force barracks at Khobar Towers in Saudi Arabia, killing twenty; the bombing of U.S. embassies in Kenya and Tanzania, killing over two hundred, most of the dead local nationals;

and the near sinking of the destroyer USS *Cole*, at Aden in 2000, killing seventeen American sailors.

45. One army-commissioned study of the service's weapons development process noted, "To produce nothing takes four years." *Final Report of the 2010 Army Acquisition Review*, January 2011, p. 19.

46. The ill-fated helicopter was the RAH-66 Comanche. Loren Thompson, "How the Army Missed Its Chance to Modernize," *Forbes*, September 27, 2011.

47. "Rumsfeld Kills Crusader Artillery Program," *USA Today*, May 8, 2002.

48. Alec Klein, "The Army's $200 Billion Makeover," *Washington Post*, December 7, 2007.

49. "$46 Billion Worth of Cancelled Programs," *DefenseTech*, July 19, 2011, http://defensetech.org/2011/07/19/46-billion-worth-of-cancelled-programs/, accessed June 25, 2012.

50. One of Rumsfeld's first major initiatives during his second tour as secretary of defense was to create the Office of Force Transformation, tasked with engineering "non-consensual revolutionary change." The phrase comes from a June 1, 2001, memo written by Vice Admiral Arthur Cebrowski, Rumsfeld's Force Transformation director, available online at the Rumsfeld Papers, http://www.rumsfeld.com, accessed June 26, 2012.

51. George W. Bush, "Address to a Joint Session of Congress," September 20, 2001.

52. In his history of the Iraq War, Thomas R. Ricks writes that the relationship between Rumsfeld and the army "had begun badly and deteriorated further with time." Ricks, *Fiasco: The American Military Adventure in Iraq* (New York, 2006), p. 68.

53. Michael R. Gordon and Bernard E. Trainor, *Cobra II: The Inside Story of the Invasion and Occupation of Iraq* (New York, 2006), p. 8.

54. Quoted in Mackubin Owens, "Marines Turned Soldiers," National Review Online, December 10, 2001.

55. Wolfowitz dismissed Shinseki's concerns as "wildly off the mark," remarking by way of a rebuttal that "it's hard to conceive that it would take more forces to provide stability in post-Saddam Iraq than it would take to conduct the war itself and to secure the surrender of Saddam's security forces and his army. Hard to imagine." George Packer, "What Washington Doesn't See in Iraq," *New Yorker*, November 24, 2003.

56. In a memoir published before the scope of the Iraq debacle was fully evident, Franks is adamant in claiming OPLAN 1003V, as it was known, as

his own personal handiwork. See Tommy Franks, *American Soldier* (New York, 2004), pp. 333, 337–41, 348–67. Later accounts, appearing after the Iraq insurgency had shredded Rumsfeld's reputation for genius, tended to tag the secretary of defense with responsibility for 1003V's defects. See, for example, Gordon and Trainor, *Cobra II*, pp. 4–5, 22–23.

57. For the provenance of the term, see Harlan K. Ullman et al., *Shock and Awe: Achieving Rapid Dominance* (Washington, D.C., 1996).

58. Phil McCombs, "Blood and Guts and Brains and Spirit," *Washington Post*, June 23, 2003.

59. Franks, *American Soldier*, pp. 367, 416.

60. Sullivan, "Delivering Decisive Victory," p. 3.

7. COPING WITH CHAOS

1. Perry Bacon, Jr., "The Revolt of the Generals," *Time*, April 16, 2006.

2. Paul D. Eaton, "For His Failures, Rumsfeld Must Go," *New York Times*, March 19, 2006.

3. Derek Thompson, "War and Peace in Thirty Seconds," theatlantic.com, January 30, 2012, http://www.theatlantic.com/business/archive/2012/01/war -and-peace-in-30-seconds-how-much-does-the-military-spend-on-ads /252222/, accessed August 12, 2012.

4. "The 10 Worst Jobs of 2012–2013: 3—Enlisted Military Soldier," http:// www.careercast.com/content/10-worst-jobs-2012-3-enlisted-military-soldier, accessed August 31, 2012. Lumberjacks and dairy farmers edged out soldiers atop the list of least attractive jobs.

5. Kim Murphy, "A Fog of Drugs and War," *Los Angeles Times*, April 7, 2012.

6. Richard A. Friedman, "Why Are We Drugging Our Soldiers?," *New York Times*, April 22, 2012.

7. Nancy Montgomery, "Reports of Family Violence, Abuse within Military Rise," *Stars and Stripes*, July 10, 2011, http://www.stripes.com/reports-of -family-violence-abuse-within-military-rise-1.148815, accessed June 28, 2012; Luiza Oleszczuk, "Divorce Rate Among Afghanistan, Iraq War Vets Increases by 42 Percent," *Christian Post*, January 2, 2012, http://www.christianpost.com /news/divorce-rate-among-afghanistan-iraq-war-vets-hits-42-percent-66195 /, accessed June 28, 2012.

8. Mike Nichols, "Study Shows Very High Rate of PTSD among Veterans," *Anxiety, Panic, & Health*, July 21, 2009, http://anxietypanichealth.com /2009/07/21/study-shows-very-high-rate-of-ptsd-among-veterans/, accessed

June 29, 2012. *PTSD*, or *post-traumatic stress disorder*, became part of the American vernacular.

9. TBI, for traumatic brain injury, was another military acronym with which Americans became familiar. Greg Zoroya, "360,000 Veterans May Have Brain Injuries," *USA Today*, March 5, 2009.

10. Robert Burns, "Military Suicides Average Nearly One a Day This Year," *Virginian-Pilot*, June 8, 2012, http://hamptonroads.com/2012/06/military-suicides-average-nearly-one-day-year, accessed June 28, 2012.

11. To understand the American national identity in 1779, with its wariness of the coercive potential of the state, the place to look was the army, George Washington's continentals mixing uneasily with various state militias. Something of that identify had survived in 1879 and even in 1979. Today it has vanished, with state troops effectively amalgamated into the regular army. Rightly or wrongly, most Americans assume that the army is politically benign; antistatists instead direct their ire at government efforts to ensure universal access to health care—an odd definition of tyranny.

12. For details, see Andrew J. Bacevich, *The New American Militarism: How Americans Are Seduced by War* (New York, updated edition 2013), chap. 2.

13. Milton Friedman, "Why Not a Volunteer Army?" December 1966, http://oll.libertyfund.org/index.php?option=com_content&task=view&id=1258&Itemid=290, accessed September 7, 2012.

14. Mary Louise Kelly, "Calculating the Cost of the War in Afghanistan," National Public Radio, October 29, 2009, http://www.npr.org/templates/story/story.php?storyId=114294746, accessed September 7, 2012.

15. Aaron Smith, "A Cost of War: Soaring Disability Benefits for Veterans," *CNN Money*, April 27, 2012, http://money.cnn.com/2012/04/27/news/economy/veterans-disability/index.htm, accessed September 9, 2012.

16. Linda J. Blimes, "Current and Projected Future Costs of Caring for Veterans of the Iraq and Afghanistan Wars," June 13, 2011, Costs of War Project, costsofwar.org/sites/default/files/ . . . /Bilmes%20Veterans%20Costs.pdf, accessed September 9, 2012.

17. "Petraeus Confirmation Hearings," *Transcripts*, January 23, 2007, http://www.cnn.com, accessed July 2, 2012.

18. By extension, COIN enthusiasts became known as "COINdinistas."

19. "Interview Col. H. R. McMaster," *Frontline*, February 21, 2006, http://www.pbs.org/wgbh/pages/frontline/insurgency/interviews/mcmaster.html, accessed July 2, 2012. McMaster was not the only commander to recognize the need for radically different methods. Another was Colonel Sean MacFar-

land. See Jim Michaels, "An Army Colonel's Gamble Pays Off In Iraq," *USA Today*, May 1, 2007.

20. For a skeptical view, offered by a retired army officer who served in Baghdad during the surge, see Douglas A. Ollivant, "Countering the New Orthodoxy: Reinterpreting Counterinsurgency in Iraq," New America Foundation, June 2011, http://www.npr.org/2011/12/16/143832121/as-the-iraq-war-ends-reassessing-the-u-s-surge, accessed July 2, 2012.

21. Kimberly Kagan, *The Surge: A Military History* (New York, 2008), p. 202.

22. Sahar Issa, "15 Die in Iraq Bombings as Nation Prepares for Arab League Summit," March 7, 2012, McClatchy Newspapers, http://www.mcclatchydc.com/2012/03/07/v-print/141124/15-die-in-iraq-bombings-as-nation.html, accessed July 2, 2012.

23. Retired Lieutenant Colonel Douglas Ollivant, quoted in Greg Jaffe, "Army at Crossroads, Facing Budget Cuts, and Uncertainty About Future Role," *Washington Post*, November 22, 2012.

24. Victor Davis Hanson, "Winning in Afghanistan: We Have Everything but a Confident Commander in Chief," (Lorain, Ohio) *Morning Journal*, November 6, 2009.

25. Greg Jaffe, "In One of Final Addresses to Army, Gates Describes His Vision for Military's Future," *Washington Post*, February 26, 2011.

26. William Kristol, "The Gates of Resignation," *Weekly Standard*, March 14, 2011.

27. John McHugh and Raymond Odierno, *2012 Army Posture: The Nation's Force of Decisive Action* (February 2012), pp. 2, 6, 17. McHugh was serving as secretary of the army.

28. Elisabeth Bumiller and Thom Shanker, "Defense Budget Cuts Would Limit Raises and Close Bases," *New York Times*, January 27, 2012.

29. As General Lloyd Austin, the last U.S. commander of the Iraq War, supervised the final extraction of U.S. forces from that country, a reporter asked what advice he had for Iraqis. Austin responded, "If I were them, I would ask for help because we are the best in the world," thereby demonstrating a remarkable absence of awareness as to what U.S. military "help" had delivered over the previous eight years. "U.S. General Sees Turbulent Future for Iraq," *Boston Globe*, November 22, 2011.

30. Elisabeth Bumiller, "West Point Is Divided on a War Doctrine's Fate," *New York Times*, May 27, 2012.

31. David Feith, "The Warrior's-Eye View of Afghanistan," *Wall Street Journal*, May 12, 2012. At the end of his tenure as Pentagon chief, Robert

Gates remarked, "I have learned a few things in four and a half years, and one of them is to try to stay away from loaded words like 'winning' and 'losing,'" thereby capturing in a single sentence the impact of Iraq and Afghanistan on Washington's expectations of what force could accomplish. Elisabeth Bumiller and Thom Shanker, "Gates Stresses the Importance of Ties with Pakistan," *New York Times*, June 16, 2011.

8. SMEDLEY AND FRIENDS

1. "Smedley Butler on Interventionism," http://www.fas.org/man/smedley.htm, accessed August 1, 2012.

2. Lee Butler, "Chaining the Nuclear Beast," October 3, 1996, http://www.wagingpeace.org/articles/1996/10/03_butler_chaining.htm, accessed August 1, 2012.

3. Lee Butler, "University of Pittsburgh Speech," May 13, 1999, http://www.wagingpeace.org/articles/1999/05/13_butler_upitt-speech.htm, accessed August 1, 2012.

4. *Attack Upon Pearl Harbor by Japanese Armed Forces,* Senate Document 159, 77th Congress, 2nd Session, January 23, 1942. The damning language providing the basis for the subsequent relief of Admiral Husband Kimmel and Lieutenant General Walter Short is found in paragraph 17 on pp. 20–21.

5. William H. Standley, "More About Pearl Harbor," *U.S. News and World Report*, April 16, 1954, pp. 40–46.

6. The report of the court of inquiry to include Admiral Moorer's endorsement is readily available online. See, for example, http://www.ussliberty.org/ncitext.htm.

7. "Findings of the Independent Commission of Inquiry into the Israeli Attack on USS Liberty, the Recall of Military Rescue Support Aircraft while the Ship was Under Attack, and the Subsequent Cover-up by the United States Government," October 22, 2003, http://www.usslibertyinquiry.com/evidence/usreports/moorer.html, accessed August 1, 2012.

8. Did Dwight D. Eisenhower develop a case of Smedley's syndrome? The case for the soldier-president as a speaker of inconvenient truths rests primarily on his Farewell Address, which identified the dangers posed by the military-industrial complex. Yet why did Ike wait until the very end of his term in office to warn of this threat to American democracy? Was it his own impending departure from public life that allowed him to recognize as a problem something that he had hitherto found tolerable?

9. Declan Walsh, "US Had 'Frighteningly Simplistic' View of Afghanistan, Says McChrystal," *Guardian*, October 7, 2011.

10. Michael Hastings, "The Runaway General," *Rolling Stone*, July 8–22, 2010.

11. At approximately the same time, another retired senior army officer weighed in with a thoughtful critique of the all-volunteer force. Lieutenant General (and former U.S. ambassador to Afghanistan) Karl W. Eikenberry stopped short of calling for conscription. See his article "Re-Assessing the All-Volunteer Force," *Washington Quarterly*, Winter 2013, pp. 7–24.

12. Josh Rogin, "McChrystal: Time to Bring Back the Draft," Foreign Policy.com, July 3, 2012, http://thecable.foreignpolicy.com/posts/2012/07/03/mcchrystal_time_to_bring_back_the_draft, accessed August 5, 2012.

9. WINNERS AND LOSERS

1. Hammering produces beneficial side effects for those at the top. During the decade of war that followed 9/11, while U.S. forces increased only modestly in overall size, the ranks of admirals and generals swelled. See "Increase in U.S. Military Ranks from 2001 to 2011," http://pogoblog.typepad.com/.a/6a00d8341c68bf53ef015393c126eb970b-pi, accessed August 30, 2012.

2. Or at least shouldn't. During the 2012 presidential campaign, a group styling itself "Special Ops OPSEC" and claiming to consist of former Navy SEALs launched an anti-Obama effort, charging the president with exploiting the bin Laden raid and leaking national security secrets for political advantage. See http://opsecteam.org/index.html, accessed August 27, 2012.

3. For a carefully documented case study of the armaments industry, see William Hartung, *Prophets of War: Lockheed Martin and the Making of the Military Industrial Complex* (New York, 2011). One illustration of the relationship between defense contractors and members of Congress: Representative Howard "Buck" McKeon (a Republican from California) chairs the House Armed Services Committee and is an ardent supporter of big military budgets. Between 2009 and 2010, his campaign committee and political action committee together took in $116,000 from defense aerospace companies; $49,000 from defense shipbuilders; $39,000 from defense electronics contractors; and another $20,000 from "miscellaneous" defense-related firms. *Open Congress*, http://www.opencongress.org/people/money/400267_Howard_McKeon, accessed August 14, 2012. McKeon receives more money from Lockheed Martin than from any other single source.

4. By 2012, the United States controlled the vast preponderance of the

global arms market. Robert Dreyfuss, "U.S. Sells Three-Fourths of Worldwide Arms," *Nation*, August 27, 2012.

5. Also encroaching on the battlefield are increasing numbers of nongovernmental organizations (NGOs) pursuing their own agendas.

6. Michael M. O'Brien, "The 'Military-Industrial Complex': Revolving Door for Retired Generals," *Warfare, Inc.*, January 5, 2011, http://americasfailure iniraq.com/2011/01/05/the-military-industrial-complex-revolving-door-of -retired-generals/, accessed August 27, 2012.

7. The benignly titled Knowledge International, located near Washington, D.C., offers one example. Its CEO is a retired air force officer, Daniel Monahan. Its "strategic advisory board" consists of McChrystal and two other retired four-stars plus one civilian. The company's self-described vision is to become the "automatic partner of choice in facilitating international transactions between the United States and the United Arab Emirates." Substantively, the transactions focus on bolstering military capabilities in the UAE and elsewhere in the Middle East. The company's Web site at http://www .knowledgeintlllc.us/ provides details, albeit cloaked in a cloud of euphemisms.

8. Commission on Wartime Contracting in Iraq and Afghanistan, *Transforming Wartime Contracting* (Washington, D.C., 2011), pp. 20, 24–25.

9. Ibid., p. 5.

10. Leo Shane III, "Report: "U.S. Wasted $60 Billion in Fraud, Abuse," *Stars and Stripes*, August 31, 2011.

11. *Transforming Wartime Contracting*, pp. 11, 32.

12. Prominent accounts include Thomas C. Bruneau, *Patriots for Profit* (Palo Alto, Calif., 2011); Shawn Engbrecht, *America's Covert Warriors* (New York, 2010); David Isenberg, *Shadow Force* (New York, 2008); Jeremy Scahill, *Blackwater* (New York, 2007); Suzanne Simons, *Master of War* (New York, 2009); and Peter Singer, *Corporate Warriors* (Ithaca, N.Y., 2004). An authoritative source on all things related to PSCs is Isenberg's excellent Web site: http://isenberg.securitycontracting.net/david-isenbergs-pmsc-writings/. But see also William D. Hartung, "The Military-Industrial Complex Revisited: Shifting Patterns of Military Contracting in the Post-9/11 Period," undated (2011), prepared under the auspices of the Brown University "Costs of War Project" and available at http://costsofwar.org/article/growth-corporate -power-and-profiteering.

13. Jonathan Werve, "Contractors Write the Rules," Center for Public Integrity, June 30, 2004, http://www.publicintegrity.org/2004/06/30/5630/ contractors-write-rules, accessed September 1, 2012.

14. The phrase *merchants of death*, which entered the lexicon of American politics in the 1930s, derives from a best-selling book by that name, written by H. C. Engelbrecht and F. C. Hanighen.

15. Report of the Special Committee on Investigation of the Munitions Industry (The Nye Report), U.S. Congress, Senate, 74th Congress, 2nd sess., February 24, 1936, pp. 3–13, https://www.mtholyoke.edu/acad/intrel/nye.htm, accessed August 24, 2012.

16. Gerald P. Nye, "U.S. Munitions Investigation," *Vital Speeches of the Day* (December 31, 1934): 217. This article reprints the text of a presentation by Nye delivered on the NBC radio network on October 3, 1934.

17. *They* very much includes senior military officers. In an investigative report describing the "revolving-door sprint from uniformed responsibilities to private paid advocacy," the *Boston Globe* determined that fully 80 percent of three- and four-star officers who retired between 2004 and 2008 found work as Pentagon consultants or with defense contractors. These officers, the *Globe*'s Bryan Bender reported, inhabit "the lucrative nexus between the defense procurement system, which spends hundreds of billions of dollars a year, and the industry that feasts on those riches." Bryan Bender, "From the Pentagon to the Private Sector," *Boston Globe*, December 26, 2010.

18. A more common term for aretai is *virtues*.

19. Theodore Westhusing, "A Beguiling Military Virtue: Honor," *Journal of Military Ethics* (2003), http://www.tandfonline.com/doi/full/10.1080/15027570310004186, accessed September 2, 2012.

20. "Born to be a warrior" is from the introduction to Westhusing's dissertation. Quoted in T. Christian Miller, "A Journey That Ended in Anguish," *Los Angeles Times*, November 27, 2005.

21. Michael Shaara, *The Killer Angels* (New York, 1974), p. xviii.

22. Undated letter to "LTC [*sic*] Westhusing." This is the anonymous letter containing the charges against USIS, made available in response to a Freedom of Information Act (FOIA) request. I thank the journalist Robert Bryce for providing me with a copy along with the other documents cited below.

23. Letter from T. S. Westhusing to Major General Fil, May 28, 2005.

24. Quoted in Miller, "A Journey That Ended in Anguish."

25. U.S. Army Criminal Investigation Command, "SUBJ: CID Report of Investigation," December 20, 2005. This thirty-seven-page report documented in detail the immediate circumstances of Westhusing's death, when and where the body was found, for example. Although noting the allegations of USIS corruption and misconduct, it did not address them.

26. Department of the Army, Office of the Inspector General, "Report of Investigation, Case 05-030," September 20, 2005.

27. Quoted in Miller, "A Journey That Ended in Anguish."

28. Greg Mitchell, "General Petraeus's Link to a Troubling Suicide in Iraq," *Nation*, June 27, 2011.

29. Matthew Moten, "Out of Order," *Foreign Affairs*, September–October 2010, pp. 2–8.

10. TRAHISON DES CLERCS

1. George Packer, "The Liberal Quandary Over Iraq," *New York Times Magazine*, December 8, 2002. Packer also interviewed Michael Walzer and David Rieff, both of whom opposed an invasion of Iraq. Neither cited concerns for the well-being of U.S. forces as part of their argument.

2. Paul Berman, "Who's for War, Who's Against It, and Why," *Slate*, February 19, 2003, http://www.slate.com/articles/news_and_politics/politics/2003/02/roll_call.html, accessed January 2, 2013.

3. Richard Cohen, "A Stranger's Wars," *Washington Post*, January 4, 2011.

4. Richard Cohen, "In Syria, It's Past Time for the United States to Act," *Washington Post*, August 14, 2012.

5. David Brooks, "The Certainty Crisis," *Weekly Standard*, March 9, 2003.

6. David Brooks, "The Phony Debate," *Weekly Standard*, March 31, 2003.

7. David Brooks, "Optimism Rediscovered," *Weekly Standard*, April 6, 2003.

8. David Brooks, "Today's Progressive Spirit," *Weekly Standard*, April 9, 2003.

9. David Brooks, "Collapse of the Dream Palaces," *Weekly Standard*, April 28, 2003.

10. Ibid.

11. Brooks, "Optimism Rediscovered."

12. David Brooks, "Boots on the Ground, Hearts on their Sleeve," *New York Times*, December 2, 2003. Brooks was by no means the only conservative writer holding this view. Adam Garfinkle, editor of the right-leaning journal *American Interest*, described "the military today as the largest repository of [the nation's] founding values." In a country beset with "internal social dysfunction," soldiers, in his view, remain committed to "industriousness, honesty, marriage and religiosity." See "A Conversation with Charles Murray," *American Interest*, March 8. 2012, http://www.the-american-interest.com/article.cfm?piece=1221, accessed August 29, 2012.

13. David Brooks, "Take a Deep Breath," *New York Times*, April 10, 2004.

14. David Brooks, "A More Humble Hawk," *New York Times*, April 17, 2004.

15. Ibid.

16. David Brooks, "Crisis of Confidence," *New York Times*, May 8, 2004.

17. David Brooks, "For Iraqis to Win, the U.S. Must Lose," *New York Times*, May 11, 2004.

18. David Brooks, "Bush's Epic Gamble," *New York Times*, May 25, 2004.

19. David Brooks, "Can We Save Iraq? No, But the Iraqis Can," *New York Times*, January 11, 2005.

20. David Brooks, "The Winnable War," *New York Times*, March 6, 2009.

21. Bill Roggio and Lisa Lundquist, "Green-on-Blue Attacks in Afghanistan: The Data," *Long War Journal*, August 23, 2012.

22. By the spring of 2012, opinion polls showed that two-thirds of Americans wanted the United States to withdraw its troops from Afghanistan. "Americans' Support for Afghan War Drops Sharply: Poll," *Reuters*, March 26, 2012, http://www.reuters.com/article/2012/03/27/us-usa-afghanistan-poll -idUSBRE82Q02K20120327, accessed August 28, 2012.

23. Notably prescient contributions include Robert W. Tucker and David C. Hendrickson, *The Imperial Temptation: The New World Order and America's Purpose* (New York, 1992); and Ronald Steel, *Temptations of a Superpower* (Cambridge, Mass., 1995).

24. For a bracing example, replete with Buchanan's trademark swipes at American supporters of Israel, see Patrick J. Buchanan, "No End to War," *American Conservative*, March 1, 2004.

25. Howard Zinn, "The Case Against War on Iraq," *Boston Globe*, August 19, 2002.

26. Immanuel Wallerstein, "The Eagle Has Crash-Landed," *Foreign Policy*, July 1, 2002.

27. Randolph Bourne, "The War and the Intellectuals," *Seven Arts*, June 1917, pp. 135–36, 143–45.

28. In the category of books, the classic remains David Frum and Richard Perle, *An End to Evil: How to Win the War on Terror* (New York, 2003).

11. DRONING ON

1. "200 U.S. Marines Join Drug War in Guatemala," *CBS News*, August 30, 2012, http://www.cbsnews.com/8301-202_162-57503167/200-u.s-marines -join-drug-war-in-guatemala/, accessed September 9, 2012.

2. For chapter and verse, see Robert Dreyfuss, *Devil's Game: How the United States Helped Unleash Fundamentalist Islam* (New York, 2005).

3. The quotations come from William M. Arkin, "The Pentagon Unleashes a Holy Warrior," *Los Angeles Times*, October 16, 2003.

4. One can only speculate regarding the fate likely to befall a U.S. high-ranking officer daring to say of Israeli prime minister Benjamin Netanyahu, "My God is a real God and his is an idol."

5. http://jerryboykin.com/.

6. The quotation is from a video clip titled "Marxism in America," October 29, 2010, http://www.youtube.com/watch?v=1QcPr9TAF1g, accessed September 16, 2012.

7. Family Research Council, Values Voter Summit 2012, Schedule of Events, http://www.valuesvotersummit.org/schedule, accessed September 18, 2012.

8. Maggie Haberman, "Romney Held Private Denver Meeting with Dobson, Bauer," *Politico*, August 3, 2012, http://www.politico.com/blogs/burns-haberman/2012/08/romney-held-private-denver-meeting-with-dobson-bauer-131076.html, accessed September 21, 2012.

9. Public Religion Research Institute, *What It Means to Be American: Attitudes Toward Increasing Diversity in America Ten Years After 9/11*, September 6, 2011, http://publicreligion.org/research/2011/09/what-it-means-to-be-american/, accessed September 22, 2012.

10. The Pentagon plans further reductions in the number of U.S. troops stationed in Europe. Donna Mills, "Force Changes in Europe to Preserve Strategic Edge," May 7, 2012, http://www.defense.gov/news/newsarticle.aspx?id=116221, accessed September 19, 2012.

11. "About U.S. Central Command," http://www.centcom.mil/about-u-s-central-command-centcom, accessed September 21, 2012.

12. "About United States Africa Command," August 2011, http://www.africom.mil/AfricomFAQs.asp, accessed September 20, 2012.

13. Akiva Eldar, "Israel's New Politics and the Fate of Palestine," *National Interest*, July–August 2012.

14. A classic example was Operation Shoshana, conducted on October 14, 1953, by the IDF's Unit 101, commanded by Ariel Sharon. Arab militants had killed an Israeli woman and her two children. In response, the IDF assaulted the Jordanian village of Qibya, killing sixty-nine while leveling forty-five houses, a school, and a mosque.

15. "Obama's Speech to Troops at Fort Bragg," *New York Times*, December 14, 2011.

16. Michael Gerson, "Obama's Iran Options," *Washington Post*, February 24, 2012.

17. Nick Turse, "A Secret War in 120 Countries: The Pentagon's New Power Elite," *TomDispatch*, August 3, 2011.

18. David Ignatius, "Deadly Drones Can't Win War on their Own," *Washington Post*, October 4, 2011.

19. Dana Priest and William M. Arkin, "Top Secret America," *Washington Post*, September 2, 2011.

20. Jo Becker and Scott Shane, "Secret 'Kill List' Proves a Test of Obama's Principles and Will," *New York Times*, May 29, 2012.

21. Alfred Kazin, *New York Jew* (New York, 1978), p. 254.

12. AMERICAN CHARACTERS

1. Alasdair MacIntyre, *After Virtue: A Study in Moral Theory* (Notre Dame, Ind., 1981), pp. 26–29. Italics in the original.

2. "A Letter from the Publisher," *Time*, January 1, 1951, p. 5.

3. "Destiny's Draftee," *Time*, January 1, 1951, pp. 16–18.

4. Ibid., p. 17.

5. "Person of the Year: The American Soldier," *Time*, January 5, 2004, p. 36.

6. Ibid., p. 5. The photographs are available at http://www.time.com/time /photogallery/0,29307,1996518_2151845,00.html, accessed September 29, 2012.

7. "Person of the Year," pp. 36, 41.

8. John Keegan, "The Making of the American G. I.," *Time*, January 5, 2004, p. 46.

9. Rudyard Kipling, "The White Man's Burden" (1899). This poem is well worth reading today. It testifies to the racist assumptions informing any attempt by a foreign army to "uplift" (or in contemporary parlance "liberate") a people said to be in need of salvation. It also warns against the lack of self-awareness that permits and sustains such benighted enterprises.

10. Charles A. Beard, "Giddy Minds and Foreign Quarrels," *Harper's*, September 1939, p. 351.

11. Wyatt Durrette and Zac Brown, "Chicken Fried," recorded in 2003 by the Zac Brown Band.

12. In retirement, Marshall refused to identify himself with either political party and never endorsed a candidate for public office. One can imagine his opinion of present-day retired senior officers who eagerly align themselves

with—and allow themselves to be used by—one candidate or another during presidential elections. See, for example, "Romney for President Announces Military Advisory Council," October 17, 2012, http://www.mittromney.com/news/press/2012/10/romney-president-announces-military-advisory-council, accessed October 23, 2012. The "council" consisted of some three hundred retired admirals and generals. Retired army General Tommy Franks explained why he was supporting Romney. "Instead of playing politics with our military, he will strengthen our defense posture by reversing the President's devastating defense cuts," Franks himself thereby using the military as a political football.

13. In 1941, Marshall actually threatened to resign as army chief of staff over what he viewed as inappropriate intrusion into matters that rightly belonged to the military. The specific issue was the organization of Officer Candidate Schools. Intent on increasing the output of these schools, Secretary of War Henry Stimson and other civilians were willing to sacrifice quality for quantity. Marshall was opposed and later recalled, "If they were going to do it—and I considered it a colossal mistake—they would do it without me." "Interview with General George C. Marshall," January 22, 1957, www.marshallfoundation.org/library/ . . . /Marshall_Interview_Tape10.pdf, accessed October 23, 2012.

14. War Department Circular 347, *Military Establishment*, August 25, 1944.

15. *Biennial Report of the Chief of Staff of the United States Army July 1, 1943 to June 30, 1945, to the Secretary of War* (New York, 1945), p. 117.

ACKNOWLEDGMENTS

I began this book intending to write a conventional narrative history of U.S. civil-military relations since World War II, an important and understudied topic. I ended up somewhere else, steered onto a different course by my growing conviction that civil-military dysfunction offers merely one symptom of a larger problem: an approach to national security at odds with democratic values that actually undermines the country's well-being. Riddled with contradictions and hypocrisy that no amount of patriotic sentimentality can disguise, our military system is broken. It produces results other than advertised. Worse, it is deeply wrong. What most Americans mistake for that system's greatest strength is actually its abiding flaw: its reliance on a force of military professionals who exist at a considerable remove from the rest of society.

So I am grateful for the forbearance displayed by my friends Sara Bershtel, Tom Engelhardt, and John Wright as I changed course, and more grateful still for their encouragement, gentle coaching, and wise counsel. Rita Quintas and Victoria Haire demonstrated admirable professionalism and efficiency in transforming manuscript into book.

Friends and acquaintances who weighed in with ideas, insights, documents, and data (but who will by no means agree with all my conclusions) include Tami Biddle, Robert Bryce, Mike Few, Doug Fitzgerald, Gian Gentile, Chris Gray, John Hall, Lawrence Kaplan, Dick Kohn, Brian Linn, Mat Moten, Barrye Price, Bill Reffett, Tom Ricks, and Paul Yingling. Thanks to one and all.

In an unexpected and unmerited gift, my colleague Andrea Berlin called my attention to the quote from Edward Gibbon that serves as the epigraph to this book.

I finished this book during a leave of absence from Boston University. I'm grateful to Dean Gina Sapiro and to my department chairs, Bill Grimes and Bruce Schulman, for letting me have the time away and for their many other kindnesses.

I spent that semester as a visiting fellow at the Kroc Institute for International Peace Studies at the University of Notre Dame. The opportunity to spend some months at that great university, which values both the Catholic tradition and intellectual excellence, was a rare privilege. I thank Scott Appleby and Mike Desch for making my stay possible. I thank Anne Riordan and members of the Kroc staff for helping to make my visit enjoyable and productive. And in a special way, I also thank the Reverend Martin Nguyen, CSC. A gifted artist and teacher, Father Martin permitted my wife, Nancy, to sit in on his undergraduate painting class. She learned a lot and had great fun. That experience made our sojourn at Notre Dame special for her as well.

INDEX

THE AMERICAN EMPIRE PROJECT

In an era of unprecedented military strength, leaders of the United States, the global hyperpower, have increasingly embraced imperial ambitions. How did this significant shift in purpose and policy come about? And what lies down the road?

The American Empire Project is a response to the changes that have occurred in America's strategic thinking as well as in its military and economic posture. Empire, long considered an offense against America's democratic heritage, now threatens to define the relationship between our country and the rest of the world. The American Empire Project publishes books that question this development, examine the origins of U.S. imperial aspirations, analyze their ramifications at home and abroad, and discuss alternatives to this dangerous trend.

The project was conceived by Tom Engelhardt and Steve Fraser, editors who are themselves historians and writers. Published by Metropolitan Books, an imprint of Henry Holt and Company, its titles include *Hegemony or Survival* and *Failed States* by Noam Chomsky, *The Blowback Trilogy* by Chalmers Johnson, *The Limits of Power* by Andrew Bacevich, *Crusade* by James Carroll, *Blood and Oil* by Michael Klare, *Dilemmas of Domination* by Walden Bello, *Devil's Game* by Robert Dreyfuss, *A Question of Torture* by Alfred McCoy, *A People's History of American Empire* by Howard Zinn, *The Complex* by Nick Turse, and *Empire's Workshop* by Greg Grandin.

For more information about the American Empire Project and for a list of forthcoming titles, please visit www.americanempire project.com